# WOMEN HEROES:

## Six Short Plays from the Women's Project

*edited by*
JULIA MILES

D1411792

APPLAUSE
THEATRE BOOK PUBLISHERS

Library of Congress Cataloguing-in-Publication Data

Women heroes.
    Contents: Colette in love / LaVonne Mueller —
Personality / Gina Wendkos and Ellen Ratner — Emma
Goldman / Jessica Litwak — Parallax / Denise Hamilton
How she played the game / Cynthia Cooper — Millie /
Susan J. Kander
    1. American drama—Women authors. 2. American drama—
20th century. 3. Heroines—Drama. I. Miles, Julia.
II. Women's Project (New York, N.Y.)
PS628.W6W66 1986 812'.54'080352042 86–25946
ISBN 0–936839–22–8

APPLAUSE THEATRE BOOK PUBLISHERS
211 W. 71st Street, New York, NY 10023
(212) 595-4735

First Applause Printing, 1987.

Second Applause Printing, 1988.

*for my granddaughter Emma—*
*and for Suzanne, Nancy, Paul and Elaine*

# THE SAMUEL BECKETT THEATRE

## THE WOMEN'S PROJECT
*of*
## THE AMERICAN PLACE THEATRE

**Wynn Handman**　　　　　　　　　**Julia Miles**
*Director*　　　　　　　　　　　*Associate Director*

*presents*

# WOMEN HEROES:
# IN PRAISE OF EXCEPTIONAL WOMEN

March 21 - April 6, 1986

*Sets by*　　　　　　*Costumes by*　　　　　　*Lighting by*
MARC D. MALAMUD and　　JUDY DEARING　　MARC D. MALAMUD
INA MAYHEW

*Projections Designer*　　　　　　*Sound Designer*
CHARLES E. HOEFLER　　　　　　GARY HARRIS

*Production Stage Manager (Series A)*　　*Production Stage Manager (Series B)*
MARY FRAN LOFTUS　　　　　　PAMELA SINGER

Casts and credits for individual plays appear on their
respective title pages.

# Contents

# INTRODUCTION

I don't remember now precisely which puncture-the-image story in what news media made me first start thinking about heroism and women. Perhaps it was, in part, living through the elation of Ferraro's political ascendance and the disappointment of her closely, minutely chronicled fall. One thing seemed likely, that in a time when political and legal advancements for women have seemed to stagnate and the media's specialization appears to be the debunking of heroes, positive, public attention on women was needed. I felt that The Women's Project, now entering its ninth year of developing and producing women playwrights and supporting and employing women directors, was particularly well equipped to provide an examination and celebration of the lives of notable, exceptional women.

For these reasons I asked the Directors Forum of The Women's Project to work with writers and create short plays—monologues or duologues—about Women Heroes. In the process of this work, the directors and writers asked many questions. What constitutes a hero? Can a hero be recognized and unsung, or must she be celebrated, acclaimed? Are the qualities of women heroes different from male heroes? (Would heroism in a man be called aggression in a woman?) And is it anachronistic to talk about heroism in the 1980s anyway?

The responses are the six plays published in this book. Intimate pieces with strong character relationships, the scripts were developed from letters, autobiographies, and the playwrights' personal observations and experiences.

The pieces include a variety: from the lyrical, fanciful COLETTE exploring her craving to write and to love and the conflict between the two to the contemporary hip woman in Gina Wendkos' and Ellen Ratner's PERSONALITY, who wryly observes "New York is a city of heroes. To become famous you have to choose who to imitate." For Denise Hamilton, Daisy Bates, the Little Rock woman who made integration a front-page issue in the 1950s, embodied heroism with her style of political savvy and courageous persistence. Her play PARALLAX shows Bates at key encounters in her life juxtaposed with the life of another, different strong woman, Rose Kennedy.

To writer Susan Kander and her director Carol Tanzman, however, the heroism of women who must endure enormous struggle just getting through each day is inspiring. MILLIE portrays such a woman and her uncelebrated courage and good humor. Writer Jessica Litwak chose the anarchist Emma Goldman, a woman whose flamboyant passions and politics played out their drama at the turn of the century. It was the parallels, though, between this woman's life and a woman of the 80s that attracted Litwak and her director Anne Bogart to her. Finally, in creating HOW SHE PLAYED THE GAME, Cynthia Cooper said that her curiosity was piqued by the lack of mention of women athletes in books purporting to cover noteworthy women. The play, a montage of famous and less well-known women athletes points up the relationship of their accomplishments in sports to other arenas where women compete and achieve.

The choices made by the directors and writers indicate as much interest in heroes of our times as of the past, in the courage and fortitude of ordinary lives as of the famous and in heroic qualities that are less traditionally celebrated. The large and enthusiastic audience indicated that the subject of heroism has resonance for women in the 80s. The six plays attest to the diversity and the strong individual feeling the subject of heroes provoked.

JULIA MILES
Director, The Women's Project
*New York City*
*June, 1986*

*Lavonne Mueller*
# COLETTE IN LOVE

Directed by Mirra Bank

Colette..................................................SHIRLEY KNIGHT
Willie, Max and Missy...........................JOHN P. CONNOLLY
Voice of Announcer......................TERRY KNICKERBOCKER
Voice of Colette's Mother...........................SUSAN STEVENS

Music Composed by Alice Eve Cohen
Lyrics Composed by Lavonne Mueller
Choreography by Joy Javits

*Characters:*

COLETTE, *age 37*
WILLY, *Colette's husband, age 47*
MISSY, *Colette's female lover, age 45, who dresses as a man*
MAX, *Colette's young lover, age 26*
*(NOTE: One male actor can play all the parts opposite* COLETTE:
WILLY, MISSY, *and* MAX.)

*Time:*

1910

ANNOUNCER: *(On tape)* And now . . . The Cat Priest you've
been waiting for . . . the bare-breasted statue drawn to the immaculate conception of fauns . . . the Egyptian Princess in orange
trunks . . . that plagiarizer of life . . . The vagabond!!

*At Rise:*

*Colette is seen standing by a chair, her back to us. She is
dressed in a loose silk robe and black stockings.*

COLETTE *(sings)*:
    When my lover
    horses around
    apes a hug
    hogs the bed
    snakes two arms away,
    or
    wolfs a kiss
    bullies lust
    ducks my lips
    and ardor strays . . .
    I sit down

put up my feet
and stare
I make myself not think
. . . of a white bear.
After a while
the only way to fight,
when I'm in love
and nothing's going right.
I
stop
just stop
and pretend I can't see
something
that doesn't need me.
When my lover
clams right up
hounds Janette
dogs LaVette
squirrels his arms away,
or
crows of *her*
bird-dogs *her*
crabs of me
and ardor strays.
I sit down
put up my feet
and stare
I make myself not think
. . . of a white bear.

COLETTE: *(Speaks above the music)* Colette, I say, you can't change the facts you don't know.

COLETTE: *(Sings)*
I sit myself down!
put up my feet!
Stare! . . .
I don't think of a white bear.

*(After the song, sparse applause. Spotlight out on Colette. Outside door we hear a jangling of bells, a scuffle; the sound of a muffled growl. Willy opens the door, smoothing his vest. He stands to one side of the stage. Colette walks to a dressing table*

*with mirror. A red bird cage hangs by the dressing table. Colette feeds crackers to the bird.)*

WILLY: So this is what you left me for?

COLETTE: I never left you, Willy. You showed me the door. *My* door. After 13 years of marriage.

WILLY: Didn't I give you Paris?

COLETTE: I'm shocking your Paris with my crude simplicity.

WILLY: I just bumped into a bear in the hall.

COLETTE: Masha. She's on before me. A clever chanteuse.

WILLY: Good. Because *you* can't sing.

COLETTE: That's why I dare to.

WILLY: Take care. The theatre's a dangerous place.

*(Willy walks to the fireplace and kicks at the logs.)*

COLETTE: What did you just do!

WILLY: I kicked the logs closer to the fire.

COLETTE: You won't get heat that way. Don't you know the fire is a living creature . . . and like any creature it wants its belly rubbed from underneath. *(She carefully smooths some logs by the fire.)* You never change.

WILLY: People are calling you . . . "danseuse et homme de théâtre."

COLETTE: *(Proudly)* A "man of the theatre."

WILLY: Why must you be . . . so much a man?

COLETTE: You, Willy, are too chichi. Why must you be so much a woman? *(Pause as Willy stares at her as she feeds the parakeet.)*

WILLY: You haven't gotten a mate for Lola?

COLETTE: No.

WILLY: A thing caged like that.

COLETTE: I would think you of all people would understand a cage.

WILLY: I understand *love.*

COLETTE: You understand *lust. (Pause)* A parakeet will ignore people if it has a mate.

WILLY: Always concerned about what loves *you.*

COLETTE: I'm concerned about what's *free.*

WILLY: Free!

COLETTE: I'm a vagabond now.

WILLY: A vagabond . . . who passionately kissed a female . . . on stage.

COLETTE: I passionately kissed an idiot—off stage.

WILLY: Don't be glib.

COLETTE: You taught me everything.

WILLY: You kissed an amphibian! In public! You know what my friends are saying?

COLETTE: At least Willy's not a cockold?

WILLY: You bared your breasts to a house full of sweaty Bohemians. All right. Ordinary bourgeois scandal. Good business.

COLETTE: I believe the reviews said . . . quote . . . "anyone who likes breasts will love them."

WILLY: This Missy thing is different. It makes me look foolish.

COLETTE: Willy, just because I blow on the fire doesn't mean I don't enjoy using the poker, too.

WILLY: The Prefect of Police has taken care of her.

COLETTE: On stage.

WILLY: I don't care what ambidextrous things you two do off stage.

COLETTE: Now . . . I can only kiss a man in front of the footlights.

WILLY: Not that I haven't enjoyed a little private "three part harmony" in love myself.

COLETTE: So your pals are more outraged by Missy than by the way you treated me for thirteen years.

WILLY: I was your teacher.

COLETTE: You locked me in a room. Made me a prisoner.

WILLY: There were . . .

COLETTE/WILLY: *(They finish the sentence together.)* . . . no bars on the window.

COLETTE: You taught me about death.

WILLY: Every morning teaches you about death . . . when you pull yourself up from the sheets after a long deep sleep.

COLETTE: You taught me unhappiness.

WILLY: Where would you be . . . happy?

COLETTE: You're always right. Joy teaches me nothing.

*(Willy goes to her and pats her on the shoulder.)*

WILLY: I didn't come here to fight. It's been six months since we've seen each other. I've nobody to give the top of my boiled eggs to in the morning.

COLETTE: I eat porridge now.

WILLY: There's nothing magic about flight. You still have to fly over every street you come to, little pear. "Ma petite poire."

COLETTE: Don't "little pear" me.

WILLY: Pear like a young moon.

COLETTE: Young? I'm three years from forty.

WILLY: Oh no you're not. *(Pause)* Willy-Willy took care of that. Don't you remember?

*(Colette is reluctant to admit remembering.)*

WILLY: Huh? *(Pause)* On your 35th birthday, we celebrated your 40th birthday *and* your 50th birthday. And got them out of the way.

COLETTE: Then . . . we made sherbert out of jam . . . and snow I scooped up from the windowsill. *(Pause)* You took me to the zoo.

WILLY: Willy-Willy knows why you like the zoo. Yes? Huh?

*(Colette gives a soft giggle)*

WILLY: You want to see the monkeys jerk off.

*(Colette begins to giggle and Willy moves up behind her pushing against her body.*

*Willy rocks her as they simulate their memory of love-making.)*

WILLY: Willy knows what you want. Willy knows . . . how fast you come. Fast as a bird's heart. Fast as a boy. I slow you down. Patience. Patience, little altar boy. Stay . . . stay. Think of all the names of your cats . . . your dogs . . . your birds . . .

COLETTE: *(Saying dreamily)* Kiki-la-Doucette . . . Toby-chien . . . Pierre Loutrec . . . Minet-Jacques . . .

WILLY: That's right . . . that's right. Hold back . . . hold back. Savor. Think of all the Claudines. Palette . . . Marie . . . Anouk . . . Polaire . . .

COLETTE: Polaire. *(Pause)* That witch.

*(Colette pulls away from Willy.)*

COLETTE: She told me they've named all the alleys on the Left Bank after your mistresses.

*(Silent pause)*

COLETTE: Is it true? *(Pause)* Well?

*(Willy thrusts out two fingers toward her.)*

COLETTE: Two alleys?

WILLY: Finger wrestle. *(Pause)* If you win, I'm guilty. If I win—innocent.

*(They each hold out two fingers and wrestle trying to bend the other's fingers.)*

WILLY: *(Struggling)* God ... but you're strong. I wish I weren't so damn fat ... I can't breathe ... I'm going to have a nose bleed ...

*(They begin to giggle and then they let go, laughing.)*

WILLY: Remember the first time I took you dancing at the Moulin Rouge?

COLETTE: My first day in Paris.

*(Willy takes her in his arms and twirls her around the room.)*

WILLY: You were wearing your mama's good shoes.

COLETTE: They were too big. I stuffed the toes with cotton.

WILLY: I kept stepping on your feet ... apologizing.

COLETTE: Don't worry. I feel nothing.

WILLY: Who has the biggest shoes in Paris—and the smallest feet?

*(They chuckle, dancing, and then lean exhausted against the dressing table. Willy sees the envelope on the table which is addressed to him.)*

WILLY: What's this? *(Reads)* Monsieur Willy.

COLETTE: Some pages I wanted to send to you.

WILLY: Trying to write on your own?

COLETTE: I've wanted to send those to you for weeks. I thought ... maybe you'd tell me ... if ...

WILLY: If what?

COLETTE: If it's ... interesting.

*(Willy rips open the envelope and takes out the pages and begins reading.)*

COLETTE: Too wordy? *(Pause)* Trite?

*(Silent pause as he reads.)*

COLETTE: It's the first draft. You know how I agonize over every sentence ...

WILLY: You agonize because you're fighting a coarse country vocabulary. *(Pause)* What did I tell you when I first read *Claudine*?"

COLETTE: Tease.

WILLY: What else?

COLETTE: Words aren't rice that swell in the cooking.

WILLY: Give me something I can eat in a reasonable length of time. *(Pause)* This needs a lot of work before I can put my name on it.

*(She turns away from him, dejected.)*

WILLY: I don't say it's without some worth. *(Pause. Goes to her.)* Little Pear ... you've been away from me six months and already you've forgotten what I taught you in thirteen years. *(Pause)* Suggest. Don't tell us everything. *(He reads from her page.)* "If there's no grace except under pressure, what about dogs running after a lost scent?" *(Pause)* What the hell does that mean? *(Pause)* Write about love ... whores ... abductors ... the common woman.

*(Colette reacts to "the common woman.")*

WILLY: The common woman is the most uncommon woman. The purer the crystal ... the less we see it. *(Pause)* I've brought you these. Pens!

*(Willy takes from his pocket a bouquet of fountain pens tied together with a bow like a bouquet of flowers.)*

WILLY: Be my "little author" again. *(Pause)* My rates are much higher now.

COLETTE: So are mine.

WILLY: You can't handle the simplest things ... like using decent paper. Scraps are for hacks. Think like a professional.

COLETTE: I've decided to be my own "ghost."

*(Willy pushes her face to the mirror.)*

WILLY: What do you see?

*(Silence)*

WILLY: Well?

*(Silence)*

WILLY: Little lines by the eyes. You do see the lines?

*(Silent pause)*

COLETTE: *(Softly)* Yes.

*(Willy lets go of the hold on her face.)*

WILLY: Do you know what it's like to be old and poor? In Paris? and alone? *(Willy writes on the mirror with lipstick.)* By ... Willy. By ... Willy. *(Pause. He stops writing.)* The "Claudine" series are a gold mine. Let her grow old with you. Claudine in the Music Hall. Claudine at forty ...

COLETTE: ... Claudine divorced. *(Pause)* Are you asking me to come back ... home?

*(Long pause)*

WILLY: I'm asking you to come back to my little band of writers.

COLETTE: You ... don't want me to live with you again?

WILLY: I'm not saying we shouldn't have our trysts.

COLETTE: You just want me as a "ghost?"

WILLY: We'll love one another in writing . . . like the old mystics loved one another in God. *(Pause)* My little pear . . . everybody wants Claudine back. My sales are down . . . we need her . . . why even the English like her. The London publishers will take as many as I can ship.

COLETTE: You know Maupassant's description of England. *(Pause)* Too many toothbrushes and not enough bidets.

WILLY: Forget England then.

COLETTE: As they say . . . "Willy *have* a lot of talent."

WILLY: I do the important editing.

COLETTE: Behind your name there's a stream sobbing. *I* do the writing!

*(She angrily rubs out all that Willy's written on the mirror.)*

WILLY: Nobody will take your books without me.

*(He tears up her recent pages.)*

COLETTE: I'll write them anyway.

*(She takes the pens from the bouquet and begins to decorate Willy with them. She puts pens behind his ears, in his hair, his jacket, his fly, his shoes.)*

COLETTE: We're like Siamese twins after the operation's failed. I'm the side bleeding.

WILLY: *(He says the following as she decorates him.)* I have a fat advance for you. *(Pause)* More than what you'd make for six months in this dump. *(Pause)* I'll throw in some new furniture. Dishes? A sixteenth century gravy boat? *(Pause)* A hat? *(Pause)* Dinner? *(Pause)* A private dinner. Just the two of us. And . . . we'll play . . . otters. In the tub. The way we used to. I'll chew on your hair . . . guggle your ears.

COLETTE: One only dies from the first man.

WILLY: I *am* the first man.

COLETTE: Today—you're the second.

*(Colette goes to the door and opens it. Willy walks out slowly. Colette slams the door.)*

WILLY: *(His voice through the door)* The poorhouse!

*(Colette paces back and forth beside the door, each time sorely tempted to touch the doorknob to let Willy back in. But she always draws her hand away.)*

WILLY: You're a slight writer. Do you hear me? *(Pause)* I know how to manage small talent.

COLETTE: I intend to grow.

WILLY: How?

COLETTE: By reading Marcel Proust.

WILLY: Who the hell's that?

*(Colette still paces by the door wanting and not wanting to open it.)*

WILLY: Do you think it was easy living with you? You and your menagerie? Flamingoes under our bed. Peacocks on top of the dishes. Chinese geese in my shaving cup. Gibbons hanging upsidedown on the drapes. Pumas, ocelots, caribou, cape penguins, clouded leopards. Your head is a zoo.

WILLY: I'll be out there every night. Waiting . . . waiting for the audience to turn on you. And when they do . . . I'll bring you decent paper to write on. And a male bird for Lola.

*(There is silence. Colette walks slowly to the dressing table and stares at herself in the mirror. Then she runs back to the door, opens it, and calls into the empty hall: "Willy!" She runs down the hall for a second, then returns. She leaves the door open and goes to her dressing table.*

*Colette looks into the mirror.)*

COLETTE: I've never been able to cry with ease, decency and fitting emotion. *(Pause)* I detest tears. They're too hard for me to conquer.

*(Colette begins to put mascara on her eyelashes and speaks to Lola the bird.)*

COLETTE: One thing that keeps me from crying, Lola, is putting mascara on my eyelashes. *(She stops with mascara and studies herself in the mirror.)* The corners of my mouth where I smile have already started to engrave a sad line. And round my throat, that triple necklace of Venus is pressed a little more deeply into my flesh every day by an invisible hand. *(Pause)* Is that a writer in there? What if . . . I can't write by myself? What if . . . they were Willy's words, after all. What if nothing were left of me but a streak of dyed color stuck to the mirror like a long muddy tear. *(Pause. To bird)* Lola, are we really vagabonds? *(Pause)* I'm beginning to talk to myself. Holding conversation with my bird . . . and the fire . . . and my own reflection. It's a habit recluses and old prisoners fall into. But I'm not like them. I'm free.

*(She continues applying more mascara and slowly the mascara brush begins to move like a pen.)*

COLETTE: *(Speaking as she tries to force out letters)* In St. Sauver, my mother, Sido, would call us to meals like one would call dogs. Dogs, however, didn't have to sit at a table and eat to the last crumb and do what they were told.

*(Colette as a child)*

MOTHER'S VOICE: Here's the box of candy from papa.

COLETTE: Can I eat it now?

MOTHER'S VOICE: Don't you want to wait till after dinner?

COLETTE: Please.

MOTHER'S VOICE: Oh . . . go ahead. *(Pause)* Minet-Cheri . . . what are you doing?

COLETTE: Running my tongue over every chocolate so I don't have to share any.

*(Colette returns to the present.)*

COLETTE: *(She speaks the following as she writes it.)* In St. Sauveur, where I was born, summer always fell into my mother's hands . . . yellow sunflowers . . . the purple iridescent irises . . . *Stops)* purple iridescent. Oh, God, how I love to seize and fix the bewitching adjective.

*(Colette starts looking anxiously for paper on her dressing table.)*

COLETTE: There is never paper. Paper!

*(Out of frustration, Colette runs her hand across a table to find it dusty. She writes in the dust.*

*Max appears in the doorway with flowers and candy.)*

COLETTE: *(Tries to write, tracing letters in the dust on the table)* I had braids long enough to lower a bucket down a well. When Willy made me cut my hair, my mother, Sido, said I had destroyed a masterpiece it had taken twenty years to create.

*(Colette becomes a child again. She stops writing.)*

COLETTE: Mama . . . mama . . .

MOTHER'S VOICE: Are you ill? Does your throat hurt?

COLETTE: No.

MOTHER'S VOICE: Then what's the matter, my jewel-all-of-gold? "Mon bijou d'or . . . "

COLETTE: I'm feeling bad . . . because I don't love anyone.

MOTHER'S VOICE: You don't love your brothers?

COLETTE: If anybody else was as good to me as they are, I'd love them just as much.

MOTHER'S VOICE: Is my Minet-Cheri saying she doesn't love her papa?

COLETTE: If anyone else read me stories and gave me sweets, I'd care just as much for them.

MOTHER'S VOICE: And you don't love mama?

COLETTE: Oh yes ... yes ... I do love you, mama.

MOTHER'S VOICE: Then go and play and stop being sad.

*(Colette returns to the present.)*

MAX: Darling, what are you doing?

COLETTE: Trying to write.

MAX: In dust? It won't last.

COLETTE: My writing isn't meant to last.

*(Max slides a box of chocolates across the floor to her. She continues to try to make letters in the dust.)*

MAX: They've all got caramel centers.

*(Colette stops, opens the candy box and begins to eat greedily. Max watches Colette as she eats dreamily.)*

MAX: I'm watching the show tonight.

COLETTE: You always do, Max.

MAX: I'm waiting for you to sing a love song to me. *(Singing)* "I love you truly" ...

*(He hands her flowers. She takes them, inhales deeply, rubs them, and plucks the petals and puts them in her mouth to chew. She puts some flower petals in Max's mouth and he laughs and chews.*

*Colette now goes to the dressing table chewing flower petals and Max follows. She puts the chocolates and flowers next to her cold cream.)*

MAX: *(He puts a small book on her head.)* A little Proust.

COLETTE: Where did you find it. *(Takes book eagerly off of her head.)*

MAX: I sent my driver to every shop.

COLETTE: I'm going to meet him, Max. Some day.

MAX: I'll arrange it. Whose his barber?

COLETTE: *(She writes Proust's name in the dust.)* Proust. *(Pause. Stares at his name)* If you're not a genius, Max, then you have to copy the courageous.

MAX: Why write copies? Relax and enjoy the original.

COLETTE: I want to write. Every free moment. In cars. On trains.

MAX: What do you mean ... trains?

COLETTE: We're going on tour.

MAX: When?

COLETTE: Next week.

MAX: I'm very good on the road. I never get sick. I don't snore.

COLETTE: Oh, yes you do.

MAX: Let me come with you.

COLETTE: No, Max.

MAX: Why do you call me . . . Max? I'm *Auguste Heriot* to everybody in Paris but you.

COLETTE: You'll be "Max" in my first book.

MAX: I want to be Auguste in your life.

COLETTE: Why do men always say the same thing as a woman at times like this?

*(Max turns away from her glumly.)*

COLETTE: Don't pout.

MAX: Then let me go with you.

COLETTE: You aren't going to cry? You know how defenseless I get . . . when a man cries.

MAX: Please.

*(Colette turns Max around to face her.)*

COLETTE: *(She pulls the cravat from his neck.)* You got this fancy scarf at the Belle Jardiniere Department store.

*(Max nods his head "yes.")*

COLETTE: I saw Marcel Proust at the Belle Jardiniere one day. At the stationery counter. He had bought some paper. The salesgirl handed it to him . . . then he saw a tray of small red pens. He picked one up and began to write on the wrapping paper. That red pen was a school child's crude beginning stick. And there he was— Proust, himself—using it . . . writing prose, hard and sweet. *(Pause)* That's what I want!

MAX: *(Eagerly)* A red pen?

COLETTE: You poor adorable dope. I want to write. To make . . . everything I sing of mine.

MAX: Everything *will* be yours. Name it! I'll get it!

COLETTE: Can you make sentences use more space than they own? Can you split a paragraph's dry center and kindle from it the page's warmth?

*(Long pause as Max stares at her)*

COLETTE: Willy can!

*(Dejected, Max turns and walks toward the door.)*

MAX: There's nothing for me to do but go away. Of course no one can make me laugh . . . the way you can. Of course I'll never smile.

COLETTE: Did I say you couldn't see me again?

MAX: *(Eagerly)* I can go with you?

COLETTE: Do you always think you'll get your way?

MAX: I told my mother all about you. *(Pause)* You'll love her. She owns a forest. Mother Ever-Cutt. She cuts and cuts and patches. She doesn't damage anything. She knows what wood is.

COLETTE: I'm glad.

MAX: I knew you would be.

COLETTE: . . . glad you've forgotten me for a moment. Tell me more about your mother.

MAX: She wants me to get married.

COLETTE: Then let yourself get married.

MAX: You're accepting me!

COLETTE: You look married already. Like the father of a big family. You're affectionate, jealous, stubborn, lazy, and pampered. You're a despot at heart and monogamous on top of it.

*(Long pause as he stares at her silently. Then)*

MAX: *(He dances around happily)* I'm all that! I'm all that! She said it. I'm all that!

COLETTE: Being egotistical, lazy, jealous and stubborn makes you want to dance?

MAX: I thought I'd never exist in your eyes. *(Pause)* go on . . . find more weakness and absurdities. Overwhelm me with my vices.

COLETTE: Max, for godsakes, don't tire me. I've work to do.

*(She begins to put somethings into a trunk.)*

MAX: What are you doing? Putting your slip and stockings in a strange man's trunk?

*(Max takes her slip and stockings back out and holds them to his chest protectively.)*

COLETTE: That's Paul's trunk. You know Paul. He plays the piano.

MAX: You're putting your private clothing next to his . . . underwear?

COLETTE: I can't afford to buy a trunk just for a few things. *(Pause)* Don't you have any sense of money at all.

*(Max holds out the pocket of his jacket and drops in Colette's stockings and slip.)*

MAX: *(Holding out pocket)* Colette's trunk.

COLETTE: I can take care of my own things.

*(She tries to get the stockings and slip back, but Max ignores her and moves away.*

*Max takes a jar of cold cream from her dressing table and throws it into the trash bucket.)*

COLETTE: You threw away my cold cream.

MAX: It's turned to cloudy oil. And smells like petrol.

*(He takes out a new fancy jar from his pocket.)*

COLETTE: *(She takes the jar from trash.)* I bought this.

*(She begins to put the old cold cream on her face.)*

MAX: *(About old cold cream)* It's melted paste.

COLETTE: ... and the color of rancid butter. But *I* bought it.

MAX: *(He tenderly wipes the old cold cream off her face and opens the fancy jar and puts on the new cream.)* Why are you so foolish about this job?

COLETTE: Max ... don't you have ... some kind of ... office?

MAX: No.

COLETTE: You do ... nothing?

MAX: Nothing.

COLETTE: Absolutely ... nothing at all?

MAX: I own some forests.

COLETTE: It's staggering.

MAX: What staggers you?

COLETTE: That anyone can live like that. No office. No factory. No rehearsals.

MAX: I want you to share it.

COLETTE: Share ... nothing?

MAX: Marry me.

COLETTE: One has to be careful *not* to fall in the direction in which one naturally leans.

MAX: Marry me. Make me happy.

*(He rubs the cream around her lips.)*

COLETTE: *(As she struggles against her feelings.)* Oh, cherubin ... please ...

MAX: You told me ... "give in to all temptation."

COLETTE: I ... told you that?

MAX: "What can we be certain of except what we hold in our arms."

*(He pulls away looking at her intently.)*

MAX: My poor little stripteaseuse.

*(He kisses her. Then he pulls away. He takes her hands and puts them under his shirt. Then he puts his hands on her breasts.)*

MAX: My nipples get hard faster than yours.

*(Silent pause)*

MAX: I'm as greedy as you. *(He throws off his coat.)* I'm always ready!

*(Max takes off his shirt and flings it on the floor.)*

MAX: Here!

*(He holds out his chest like breasts)*

COLETTE: My . . . dapper stripteaseuse.

*(Colette leads him to the divan.)*

*(She pulls him down to the sofa in an embrace. As they touch the sofa several cats protest. Colette shoos them away with one hand while guiding Max to her with the other.*

*As they are embraced in love, music comes up very softly . . . Passage of time . . . then gradually the music gets a little louder . . . and a little louder.)*

COLETTE: You have to let me go now. Don't you hear the little bear . . . shaking her harness bells and crooning . . . I'm next.

*(Max slowly pulls away, rubbing her arms.*

*She stands and goes to a dressing screen. Max gives her a fast kiss on the cheek and starts for the door.)*

COLETTE: Leave by the window.

MAX: By . . . what window?

COLETTE: *(Points off stage)* We're only one floor up.

MAX: But what will people on the street think?

COLETTE: I don't care about them.

*(Max exits to the window side of the stage as Colette stands watching him.)*

MAX: *(From off stage)* Marry me!

COLETTE: Jump! *(Pause as he does this)* Excellent. Goodbye. *(She turns and goes behind the dressing screen and takes off her robe. She puts on a pair of man's black trousers and a white tux shirt. She comes out from behind the screen putting on a man's hat.*

*Colette comes center stage and stands by a chair. She puts one leg up on the chair.)*

COLETTE: *(Sings)*

If I were Proust
I would want to be
a hot item

and throw rowdy orgies
with music hall girls
in some yellow silk cabana by the sea.
If I were Proust
I would not stick myself
to some cork-lined room
but would make wanton love
to a hack
to a bad singer in black.

*(The music fades and Colette stops singing and takes off her hat and now sits on the chair and looks around the audience.*

*Her words from the song are heard softly over a speaker to show us she is really singing as she says the following thoughts out loud.)*

COLETTE: Ahhhh . . . a nice Saturday house.

*(Pause)*

A thick reddish smoke in the air . . . stale tobacco, twopenny cigars smoked down too far.

COLETTE: Well, look at the liquid Jezebel in the first row.

*(Pause)*

You were Willy's mistress a long time ago. You didn't expect to see me tonight. Ahhh, you're afraid of confronting me like this. But it's not me you fear, little idiot. It's your own memories of Willy.

*(Pause)*

And now, here you are. In the front row. Your chair's so close to the stage I can see where you dye your hair to hide the gray. And . . . you've aged in the last four years.

*(Pause)*

Remember how Willy used to confide you to my care? For whole days at a time? He commanded me not to bring you back to him until seven o'clock. Those were some tete-a-tetes we had. Two betrayed women who hated each other . . . trying to get through long lonely afternoons.

*(Pause. Looks around)*

So this is the way my love life goes. Max over there in the first stall . . . Max, wanting me to sing him a wedding song.

*(Pause)*

Missy in the fourth box . . . Missy, out there waiting for my nerves to show so she can throw me a kiss and calm me.

*(Pause)*

And Willy in the upper circle . . . Willy, who is banking on me to fail.

*(Pause)*

Last night I dreamed I had never been in love and for once I rested as though I were in a sweet soothing sleep.

*(She stands and puts on her hat.)*

COLETTE: *(Singing)*

> If I were Proust
> I'd go to the Boulevard
> at two in the afternoon
> in red leotards
> to hum street songs
> for matrons
> and old men.
> If I were Proust
> I would sit
> in an all night theatre
> in a wide straw hat
> waiting
> to meet a stripteaseuse like me
> the kind of writer I could be
> if I were loved by a Proust
> like me.

*(The spotlight goes out on Colette.*

*A few people clap limply. Some people hiss and boo.*

*Colette sits in the chair, takes scraps of writing paper from her pocket and tries to write. After a pause, Missy appears at the dressing room door in her usual male clothing. She is smoking a cigar.)*

MISSY: What's Proust to them? Nobody likes that song.

COLETTE: I do, Missy.

MISSY: It hurts me when they hiss at you.

COLETTE: Tomorrow I'll sing sorrowful winter songs. And they'll love me.

MISSY: I want them to love you every night.

COLETTE: What's the excitement in that?

*(Missy goes to Colette and kisses her on the neck.)*

MISSY: Your rash is back.

*(Colette continues writing.)*

*(Missy goes to dressing table and gets a can of talcum and returns to sprinkle it on Colette's shoulders.)*

MISSY: I never see you smoking any more.

COLETTE: I started to enjoy it, so I began to be distrustful.

MISSY: You've got it too hot in here.

COLETTE: I love humidity. It satisfies something vegetable in me.

MISSY: This isn't talcum.

COLETTE: Powdered sugar. *(Colette reaches up and takes some on her fingers and eats it.)*

*(Missy starts to brush off the powdered sugar from Colette's shoulder, but Colette stops her. Colette continues to write and intermittently tastes the powdered sugar on her shoulders.*

*Missy returns the sugar/talcum to the dressing table and then goes to Lola the bird. Missy begins to feed Lola a cracker.)*

MISSY: When I come into a room when you're alone with your bird . . . and your cats . . . I feel I'm committing an indiscretion. Some day you'll retire into a jungle.

COLETTE: *(Doodles isolated letters)* Missy, the jungle's here. The letter "S" standing on end like a protecting serpent. "Q" resting on its tail.

MISSY: Have you changed Lola's water?

*(Silence as Colette tries to write.)*

MISSY: *(To bird)* Poor little Lola . . . you're lonely.

COLETTE: Willy's threatened to get her a mate.

MISSY: Not a coocoo like himself, I hope. *(Looking around)* The cat dishes are empty. I was going to bring them ham slices, but I'm broke.

*(Pause)*

Father stopped my allowance. *(Pinching off bits of bread to put in the cat dishes)* I'll have to watch my money now. I even canceled a cutaway coat I ordered—garnet velvet. It was such a wonderful pompadou whim.

*(Pause)*

Have you eaten?

COLETTE: *(Says as she struggles to write)* Ten chocolates . . . 8 nougats . . . petits fours . . . fudge.

MISSY: I brought some fresh bread and butter. I wish you'd eat properly.

*(Missy throws her cigar on the floor and stamps on it.)*

MISSY: Why can't you settle down. And get married. You're so much more sensible and affectionate when you're married.

*(Missy goes to Colette and feeds her bits of bread as Colette struggles to write.)*

COLETTE: The crowning glory of a wife's career is to be divorced.

MISSY: Don't be tough. Vulgarity's for women who have no talent.

COLETTE: You suggest marriage when you know what Willy did to me.

MISSY: He taught you to write.

*(Missy stops feeding Colette and puts the bread in her pocket.)*

COLETTE: I've only finished one paragraph today.

*(Colette crumbles up a page of writing and throws it on the floor. She goes to the divan and throws herself face down on it.)*

COLETTE: I can't do it by myself.

*(Missy takes the crumbled paper from the floor, smoothes it out and reads it.)*

MISSY: *(Reading)* My mother's back garden was invisible to passersby, swathed in a mantle of wisteria and begonia too heavy for the trellis. She would scan the thick green clumps and raising her head, fling her call into the air: "Children? Where are the children? Les enfants. Ou sont les enfants?"

*(Pause)*

Can Willy take this away? *(Pause)* Can he?

*(Missy rubs Colette's back.)*

MISSY: You should laugh at him. *(Pause)* You now what Willy does when he goes into train compartments marked "women only"? And the conductor demands that he come out?

*(Pause)*

Willy screeches: "But I'm Marquise de Missy."

*(Pause)*

Can you hate a clown?

COLETTE: I still love the clown. After everything he's done to me. The stink of Willy will be on every word I write.

*(Missy pulls Colette close to her and holds her. After a pause)*

MISSY: Have hope for the past . . . that it will have been all right. *(Pause)* And don't make a dragon out of your life—just so you can fight it.

*(Pause as Missy comforts Colette.)*

MISSY: Now, I have a surprise. *(She takes something from her pocket.)* I've made myself a moustache—with the help of a certain poodle's tail.

COLETTE: Who?

MISSY: Mimi . . . you know her. She performs with the German acrobats. *(Missy holds the mustache up to her lip.)* Like it?

COLETTE: Oh, yes.

MISSY: I'll wear it to see you off tomorrow morning.

COLETTE: I'm lonely for you already.

MISSY: We'll write each other witty letters.

COLETTE: Witty letters are addressed to strangers—not to one's nearest.

*(A flourish call of bugles is heard.)*

COLETTE: *(Begins to get up from the divan)* The high wire act. You know I start dressing on their bugles.

MISSY: You're always ready too soon, you poor boob of an amateur.

*(Missy begins to feed Colette with pinches of bread.)*

MISSY: I'll organize everything, darling, so you can write more. I'll file your papers . . . and number each page when you finish it. I can recopy your stories. Your handwriting's so sloppy.

*(Colette grabs the bread from Missy and breaks off a big chunk and stuffs it in Missy's mouth to gag her.)*

COLETTE: *I'll* keep my papers in order. I'll number the pages. I'll copy my own stories. *(Pause)* I damn well mean to try!

*(Colette up from the divan and goes to the dressing table. Missy follows.)*

COLETTE: *(She looks at herself, brushes her hair quickly.)* I have to change. I've been sweating in this like three furniture movers.

MISSY: *(Kissing Colette s arm)* Yes. The smell of man.

*(Pause)*

Get ready darling. Then after the show, come back to me . . . like a cat goes back to its favorite cushion when its tired after having been out too long.

*(Colette goes behind the dressing screen. Missy exits.)*

COLETTE: *(Speaking from behind the screen)* You know what I did yesterday? My skirt was so worn in one place that I took out pen and ink and inked over the threadbare patch.

*(Pause)* Maybe . . . maybe . . . Lola and I do need a husband. Man . . . my dear enemy.

*(Pause)* Darling, fetch me a drink. I know it's forbidden . . . we're not supposed to drink before working time, but just a little pale absinthe.  Please . . . Missy . . .

*(Colette out from behind the dressing screen. She see that Missy has gone. She goes to her dressing table, takes out a blue exercise book, pauses to listen.)*

COLETTE: The little bear is on. I'm next. But there's still a few minutes.

*(She speaks as she stares at paper.)*

My mother said: "You are my golden sun. When you come into the room, it grows lighter."

*(Colette pauses then speaks the following as she writes.)*

COLETTE:  In St. Sauveur, the clown-face woodpeckers searched my mother's trees. She liked no music but the croaking of ravens. Shadows leaned against her kitchen door like tired tramps.

*(Pause)*

I belong to a country I've abandoned.

*(Drum roll announcing Colette's act)*

COLETTE: *(She stands)* Mama . . . I've left Willy.

MOTHER'S VOICE:  I took you on a picnic. After running all afternoon in the mint and wild garlic, you spread out on the grass to sleep, tired of the sun.

COLETTE: I'm trying to be free.

MOTHER'S VOICE: Let me read to you, Minet-Cheri.

COLETTE: Yes, mama. Read me the story again about the old Burgundy prisoner.

MOTHER'S VOICE: On his first day home, he kept walking back and forth over the threshold—hour after hour. To remind himself of freedom. *(Pause)*

MOTHER'S VOICE:  . . . back and forth . . . back and forth . . . *(Faintly)* . . . back and forth.

*(Willy now comes down the aisle of the theatre to the edge of the stage. He puts a new birdcage and a stack of writing paper on the edge of the stage.*

*Colette looks at the new birdcage, at Lola, then at the doorway. Colette goes to the door and walks back and forth through it. Then she stops and goes to Willy and hands him back the paper and the new cage. She watches him exit down the main aisle of the theatre.*

*Drum roll. Spotlight on the door.*

*Colette goes to stand inside the door frame. She holds out her arms to each side of the door.)*

ANNOUNCER: And now . . . from St. Sauver . . . by way of Paris . . . the small town girl stiff with Sunday . . . the tart . . . intellectual . . . hoofer . . . tramp . . . scarecrow lover . . . muse's pet . . .

COLETTE: *(In a jubilant cry of freedom)* Colette!

THE END

*Gina Wendkos and Ellen Ratner*

# PERSONALITY

Co-Directed by Gina Wendkos and Richard Press
Performed by ELLEN RATNER

*Scene:*

> *Lights up on woman sitting in chair, downstage, lighting ciga-*
> *rette. Her posture and accent is that of "Lorette," her mother, a*
> *Jewish cartoon figure of 54 years old. Lorette speaks to imagi-*
> *nary husband "Sol." He is stage left and never seen. Lorette*
> *speaks very stylized New York Jewishese.*

LORETTE: Ellen, in America if you are not famous you are
nothing more than a slimy cockroach, and you are quickly forgotten.
When you are famous life is easy
everyone wants to be your friend
they invite you to the right parties
they ask your opinion
they eat what you eat
they say what you say, they even dance like you dance.
Basically it is all of you that is enviable,
your hair
your smile
your figure
your face
your personality
everything.
Sol, get me another ashtray. Look at this masugana daughter
walking away. With her personality she should be listening. Ellen
are you listening to me? Ellen!
> *(With a slight change in posture woman becomes Ellen,*
> *Lorette's daughter. She is 30 years old, no strong accent.)*

ELLEN: Confidence? Please, that's easy ... let's face it.
We're living in New York City. Right? City of heroes. Isn't
everyone here exactly the kind of person you want to be? Sometimes when I get up in the morning, I don't even know what clothes
to put on ... the choices here are so enormous. Who should I be?
You have to remember, when you dress like one camp, you auto-
matically alienate another ... and in these modern times that's a
problem. I mean, I get along. I don't have all that much of a
problem making friends. No, really I don't. In fact at the restaurant

where I work it's real easy to meet people, and poeple like me because I'm friendly. They say, "Hi Ellen, how's life?", and I say "Hi gang, life is swell." You see that's an attitude you have to have in N.Y.C., that things are swell. Just say it with me, things are swell. Things are swell. See? If you say it enough, it starts to have a nice ring to it. Things are swell. And when things aren't, if you want my opinion, say they are anyway. Because that's exactly what gets you over. There isn't a single person in this city that wants to hear, things suck. So just say like me, "things are swell," give a cheerful smile, say "Hi Gang!" And you keep all your secrets to yourself. *(Pause)* Another lesson? Only tell people secrets you really want everyone to know. Like for instance, say "Hey Jane, you wanna hear a secret?" She'll say "Yeah, yeah, yeah, yeah, yeah." And then tell her something that you'd tell anyone. This way she thinks she's special ... but she'll never have anything *(phone ring)* on you.

*(Phone call #1)*

Hello, hi Ma. Yes, I got the invitation. They're real nice ... is Eileen happy with them? Well, I'm not sure yet ... can't I come alone? No one right now ... there is this one guy, but ... well, I don't think it's really right, cause we just met ... yeah, he's real nice ... I'm sure he works ... I don't know ... I didn't ask him ... if we see each other one more time I'll ask him ... about 5'11" maybe 6'. Yeah, he's handsome ... like a Robert deNiro type. Ma, what is wrong with Italian for Chrissake? Why would that embarrass you, tell me. Why?

*(Switch to LORETTE)*

Sol, she's bringing a greasy Italian to the wedding. I remember a few years ago, there was this bar mitsvah. Ellen was a little heavy then. So I said to her whatever you do, do not wear white. What color do you think she wore? White. She looked like a blimp. P.S. do you know to this day people from that bar mitsvah still ask me, how is Ellen? Is she still a little chunky?

*(Switch to ELLEN)*

The thing I always wanted to be called was a HOT BITCH. There was something very sexy, very dirty, very Italian about that. I wanted it. I wanted to wake up one morning with some guy and hear him on the phone. Some guy named Jake or Rick. I wanted to lie in bed, leave the sheets draped so that only my thighs were covered. I'd lie there pretending to be asleep, but really I've got it arranged so I look takeable. Very takeable. I'll move my hair so that it covers the pillow but still shows my face and I'd lift up my hips so my waist looks smaller just like in the photos and I'll listen to this Jake or Rick or Tony guy on the phone, talking to one of his friends. "Hey, buddy, how ya doin'? Listen I've got this really hot bitch here. Yeah, she steams. Huh? Her name is Ellen, and she looks like a Sophia Loren type. One of those round hot Italians. Nah, met her on the street and I just wanted her. I couldn't stay away. So I went up to her and said I've never seen anyone like you. I've never smelled anyone like you, I've never wanted anyone like you, and she just looked at me and smiled. I knew I could touch her and I knew once I touched her I'd never leave. Yeah, she's really something else. I could get lost in her hair alone, it's so long and gets everywhere but I want my mouth on it." That's the kind of conversation I imagine. Then this Jake or Rick or Tony guy would come in and see me posed like that. Even if he knows it's arranged he'll like it. He'll come in and pull the sheet back and I'll stay still and he'll just look at me and I can feel his eyes, his wanting me, so I'll let out a little moan so he'll know I'm awake. *(Phone ring)* Fuck the personality for a minute. Sometimes I want to be wanted just for the way I walk.

*(Phone call #2)*

Hello. Hi, Mom, I'm getting ready ... he's pickin' me up around eight ... No I'm not wearing my hair up ... I was thinkin' about that orange sweater and blue skirt ... yes, it still fits. Some French restaurant ... I'll be fine ... that was a long time ago ... don't do that, Mom, those are snails ... chicken in red wine ... vichyssoise, vichyssoise, is cold potato soup, can we stop this now? If I don't know anything I'll just point to it on the menu ... Mom, au revoir Mom, au revoir.

*(Switch to* LORETTE*)*

There are a lot of pretty girls in this world, a lot of competition. So, it would seem to me that, it would be very difficult, if you're not so good looking, to get a man to take care of you. I gold Ellen she should get a skill. I worked in an office when I met Sol. It's 7:30. My favorite show is on, "Wheel of Fortune." I love this show. They give you the letters and you have to figure out the phrase. There she is, Vanna White, the hostess, I love the way she turns those letters over, ding, ding, ding, ding, ding. Her lipstick is always perfect. Her hair doesn't even move. I told Ellen she should go on this show, she'd win 25,000 dollars, put it in the bank and she'd be set for life.

*(Switch to* ELLEN*)*

Money. Sure, got lots of it. Can't you tell? Don't I have that certain swagger that a New York woman has? It's a casual stride. It's a slow walk, but one that gets where it has to be. Slow yet quick. Y'know what I mean? I never understood how to have money . . . the idea of becoming a career girl always seemed so stupid to me . . . of all the stupid advances of women, that has got to be the worst. Sure Lois Lane, she's got a byline in the Metro paper, she cooks quick dinners and still has time to fly all night with her boyfriend. What the hell is so liberating about leaving the home and kids for some stupid desk job . . . some idiot paper work job that men used to do? But now women get to because we're oh, so advanced. That's bullshit. So that's why I never figured out how to have money, and in this city that's ridiculous, because that's exactly how people judge you here. By your apartment, by your clothes, by your shoes. Shoes are very important because they're so expensive, the good ones, and the bad ones are a dead giveaway that you're piss poor. So I do what any noncareer, nonmarried girl would do, spend forty bucks for expensive sneakers and then everyone will think that you can afford expensive shoes . . . but choose not to. Money. Growing up it wasn't hip to want it. Who knew that would only be a 10-minute trend. Now every street bum, every street scum, every low life standing on the corner has more cash than I have. And I haven't got the first clue. *(Pause) (Phone rings)*

*(Phone call #3)*

Hello, Hi Mom. Yeah, we had a great time. Yes. Great. We had a nice dinner and expresso, and then we went to this other place for drinks and it was just sort of terrific. Y'know one of those really fun nights, where everything went well. Mom, why do you ask me stuff like that? Cause I think it's sort of personal. No, I am not ashamed . . . it's just really personal. So what if he did? Times have changed. First date, second date, third date, what difference does it make? What if he did sleep over, what does that mean? Huh Mom, what does that mean?

*(Switch to* LORETTE*)*

Sol and I both agreed that the number is four. Four men is the limit for a woman to sleep with before she gets a bad reputation. Number one is the one you lost your virginity to; it was summer, he had a nice car. Number two, that one's because you kind of forgot what it was like the first time. You were a little nervous. The third one is like practice makes perfect. You're preparing yourself for number four, the one you're gonna marry. I tell Ellen the number is four. After that they call you a used car.

*(Switch to* ELLEN*)*

Oh yeah, a woman . . . do you get it? You know, that other group that's not a man but also not a teenager. No giggling allowed. Pretty strict rules in this woman biz. As a kid it never mattered, you could climb trees and giggle. But now only one of those attitudes is allowed or you don't get over. It's OK. If you want to act tough . . . "HEY, WHAT THE FUCK YOU MEAN" . . . then people know who you are . . . on, she's a tough broad, watch out. And it's cool if you have pert breasts and giggle, then people know the score. But try having pert breasts, saying "FUCK OFF" and giggling. People look at you like, "Huh, aren't you breaking a few rules?" If you're the tough type you're supposed to have saggy tits used mainly for childbearing . . . and if you're the giggling type your breasts are meant for handling, open invitation . . . but try having saggy tits and giggling . . . the game's up. I mean, these are invisible rules. But watch. Look out, and see if I'm not right, giggling is forgivgn if the girl is hot, and tough is forgiven if she isn't. But make a sexy girl tough and no one knows the right response. Then all of a sudden men start stuttering and tripping and losing their grip. All of a sudden you're a prickteaser cause their dicks are getting hard, and they say, "WHY THE SHIT DOES SHE HAVE TO WEAR THOSE HEELS?" you hear them say. But the giggly types can with no problem. So you see, some days I'm a giggly type. I laugh at everything. I'm coy. I'm sweet. I'm available. And other days I'm a tough broad. Take no shit. Gotta get the job done, gotta get it going. But my tits stay the same. That's where things get pretty confusing for the world at large.

*(*LORETTE *escalates to screaming fit to imaginary Sol)*

Ellen is not very domestic. She does not cook. She does not clean. I remember a couple of years ago this Mother's Day. Sol do you remember this Mother's Day. Eileen bought me this beautiful purple robe. Very lovely, very flowing. Ellen had no money so she decided to come over and cook for the family. So she got here about three hours early and she chased us all out of the kitchen and she cooked. The hours later dinner was ready. Do you know what it was? Pasta and a salad. Three hours. Pasta and a salad. And you should've seen the mess the kitchen was in. And have you ever seen Ellen's bathroom? You could vomit. There's always a pound of gunk in the soap dish. She keeps her towels on the floor, gets out of the shower and wipes herself with them. And her bathtub! I don't think she's ever cleaned it since she moved into her apartment. I tell her it's very simple, after you finish, you take a glass of water and you rinse it out. My favorite is her tampax box, she leaves it out in the middle of the floor so "Hey, everybody, Ellen's got her period!"

*(Switch to* ELLEN*)*

What is it? It's so many things . . . things that I can't even feel. Things that are so invisible, things that don't have molecules. Can you imagine something without atoms? Something that doesn't have any cells. Something that shakes like jello when you touch it, but is so strong it stays like a rock in the bottom of the ocean. something like a huge couch, in the middle of your living room. You have to walk around it. You have to vacuum around it, cause it's too heavy to budge. Magazines fall under it. Phone bills drop behind it. These things get lost. They stay hidden. Just cause of this big, stupid, clumsy couch in the middle of your already crowded living room. Every time you sip coffee, or every time you eat coffee cake, some of the coffee spills onto the couch, the fabric gets stained. The crumbs fall into the cushions . . . they get imbedded and then dust keeps them glued into the cracks and holes. Cigarettes burn tiny holes from fallen ashes. Sometimes your cat pees right in the middle of it and there's nothing you can do about it . . . because it's this big, clumsy, stupid couch sitting in the middle of your already crowded living room. And that living room, that living room is like me. My legs, my arms, my hair, all things that I'm always tripping over. Things that I can't get away from. Things that are always in my way, and the couch, the couch is my heart. Stuck right in the middle with nowhere to go. Always trying to get around it. Always trying to pick out those dust balls. But instead I just keep putting my finger into those tiny cigarette holes and making them bigger and bigger and bigger, until the hole is bigger than the couch, and then the hole takes up my livingroom.

*(Switch to* LORETTE*)*

Our youngest daughter, Eileen is getting married. So we went to Andre's to look for a dress. Does my daughter want a dress from Andre's? No. She says to me "Mom, I want a Norma Kamuli, Kamali. I don't know what this is. So we go to the showroom. Every dress looked like a sweat shirt with shoulder pads. I'm spending $30,000 on my daughter's wedding and she wants to get married in a sweat shirt. O.K., times have changed. By the way, she's marrying a very, very nice boy from a well-to-do family in Texas. So she says to me the other day, "Mom, I want to wear white cowboy boots with my gown." Are you listening to this? Sol, could you get me a glass of water, I'm a little parched. Now our oldest daughter, Ellen. Ellen, Ellen, Ellen. She's thirty years old. She doesn't know what she wants to do with her life. When I was her age, I had two children, a home I could basically call my own and I was president of the P.T.A., and I started a Hadassah unit out here. Sol tell them how much money we raised for the Hadassah. Just tell them. 40,000 dollars. 40,000 dollars. Ellen never has any money. I told her a good job for her is word processing. You work in an office, you meet nice people. She won't investigate it. She's lazy and she's sloppy. She is not pretty per se. What man is gonna want her? You know what her problem is? She is not aware. In my day, you see Jackie with pillbox hat—you get pillbox hat. I'm telling you Sol, Eileen is like me and Ellen is like you. Ellen would never have had such a lousy personality if she listened to me. What do you mean by that? Oh, well you've been a great example. How many months have you been out of work? Huh? Thank God you paid for this wedding before you lost your job. I'm used to twenty years of not having you around the house. Now you're here all the time. You're driving me crazy. I don't want to hear it. Don't tell me your problems. You sit on your ass all day. Hey, hey, hey—don't talk to me like that. You have a lot of nerve. I'm not one of those no good lazy friends of yours. Sol you're dead to me. You're dead to me.

*(Switch to* ELLEN*)*

And the tension, the tension. It winds me up so bad. The Puerto Ricans on the street yell "Hey, baby, I really wanna suck your thing" . . . the Puerto Ricans, they tell me what they want. I say, hey mofo, I'm pissed off. Real pissed off. So pissed off that I want to start a fight. I'm so pissed off that one more word out of you and acid's on your face. One more word out of you and I'll blow your brains off. One more word out of you and I can see myself careening like a lion at a tiny spider. I'm gonna eat that tiny spider and I'm gonna slowly make him my saliva, until I can feel every scrawny leg on my wet tongue and I munch 'em up. That's what I'm gonna do. To all the spiders. Because, you see, I'm generally the spider, that ugly, skinny little thing waiting to get licked and bitten by all the Puerto Ricans on the street. All the

Frenchmen in the cafes, all the Italians in the gondolas, all the Indians on the reservations, all the children hiding under their swings, all the old people hiding under wrinkles. It's them, all of them . . . whispering things to me . . . things they know I want to hear . . . things that will make me like them. Things that will cause me to be them, watch them, imitate them, taste them, need them. Need them so much so that I swallow their secrets and call them my own. Repeat their name and feel in on my tongue as it becomes me. Steal their clothes, and when I put my hand in their pocket . . . it is my cigarettes *(Phone rings)*, kleenex, my keys, that I pull out. What they have whispered to me, I shout back so quickly, so strongly that I believe it.

*(Phone call #4)*

Hello. No, Ma, he didn't call . . . how the fuck do I know? Huh, are you satisfied . . . you said he wouldn't and he didn't. So do you have the balloons out?? Are you throwing a party? Huh? Did you make a fuckin' cake while you're at it? No, no! I'll say whatever I want at this fucking point. I am sick and tired of hearing how I should do it, how I should way it, how I should act it . . . are you gonna show me how to fuck, too? Who are they, who are them? Bullshit! My personality, Ma. WHAT IS WRONG WITH MY PERSONALITY? WHO DO YOU WANT ME TO BE? HUH? WHO?

GAME SHOW LADY *(Midwest accent):* I'm going to be on the 10,000 Dollar Pyramid. I'm so excited. You see I read everything. Books, magazines, backs of cereal boxes. Just ask me anything. (ANNOUNCER'S VOICE) "What is the capital of Burma?" *(buzz)* "Rangoon." "How does the whojoo bird protect itself?" "Its fur inflates into a protective covering." I know it all. Animal, vegetable, and mineral. They also like me on TV because I have a bubbly personality. So when they say, "You have won a trip to Puerta Viarta," *(Screams)* Puerta Viarta! (ELLEN *jumps up from sitting— stage flooded in wash)* Does that come with the Samsonite? Oh my god! I know just what I'm going to wear . . . my red dress. You can't wear stripes or plaids because they bleed, that's TV talk. I love TV talk. And I'm going to get my hair done and buy new shoes, then watch out America. I'm gonna take you for every red cent you have.

SPANISH CHA-CHA GIRL *(Low-class Spanish accent):* Maria, conyo, Julio, si. I love this place. Mongo Santa Maria *(dances and sings)* Julio get me a gin and tonic. Julio, he's my boyfriend. He's got the best ass in this place. He wears his pants real tight, too. He likes it when I wear this red band-aid top. But when you're dancing it keeps falling down so you have to keep a whooping and a whooping. Julio and I are going to be in a contest and we're going to win. Julio thinks the prize is fifty dollars but I'm going to surprise him. The prize is going to be me. And I'm not going to use birth control. So that way I get the ring, the car, and Julio.

VIDEO GIRL *(Brooklynese accent):* Hey, hi guys, hi Rusty. How ya doin'? Slap me five. Sally, Sally you look gorgeous. Let me see this dress. Hey, who's the squirt at my machine? Looks right for you Sal, about nine or ten years old. Hi Pee Wee. How ya doin'? Oh boy, 500 points, I don't believe it. Better watch out you're gonna be eaten. Better watch out. Told you. You're history. O.K. the champ is here. *(Makes the sound of Pac Man)* See I do this game better than I know anything else. See. All these people are gonna gather round me now. Watch. Here somes that Reggie guy. He's cute, but obnoxious. Hi Reggie. I cut last period. School is boring. Yeah, I got 50,000 points and I've only been here 30 seconds. O.K. I'll see you around. Creep. People say I could go pro at this game. Then I could quit school. What do I have to know about the Boston Tea Party? I don't even drink tea.

MISS AMERICA *(Dumb Southern drawl):* *(Sings "Here She Comes Miss America")* Thank you all, thank you so much. It's been a wonderful year being Miss America. And now I am giving my crown to the new Miss America. Whoever she is I'm sure she won't have a year like I've had. I won a college scholarship. . . . What? . . . and a movie contract . . . What? . . . and a trip around the world . . . the crown, I know. I traveled around the world and saw so many underprivileged people. You should see how these poor darlin's live. They have animals right in the house, this yak came right up to the table and ate off it. It was disgusting. And the men have the longest *(Said in silence)* you ever saw. I remember we were in some remote part of Africa and there was this little boy and he didn't have any shoes. Well my heart was just pained, so, I turned to my manager and said "What can we do?" Well, he turned to me and said "Karen Ann Sue, I ain't doing shit." So I turned to that little native and said *(Sings)* "We are the world, we are the children." That's just one of the many things I've done as Miss America. Let's hope the new Miss A. will be as generous and kind. Thank you.

HOUSEWIFE *(Nancy Reagan accent):* I take pride in the things I do. Every single one of them. Some women keep their homes in horrible condition. They leave the butter out and it sours. They serve jelly from the jar and it develops and unsightly crust around the rim. Oh yes, and they use paper napkins. REALLY! Paper napkins. *(Screams at kids)* TOMMY, JIMMY, GET AWAY FROM THAT REFRIGERATOR BEFORE I CUT YOUR HANDS OFF. I use cloth napkins only. I have several patterns. Checkers, stripes, floral prints, even polka dots. But of course polka dots I only use in summer. Really, polka dots in winter. *(Screams at kids)* DID YOU HEAR WHAT I SAID? DID YOU HEAR WHAT I SAID? GET UPSTAIRS WITH YOUR BROTHER. Ah, summertime, such a peaceful season. The little misters are in camp. The birds are in the yard. Robert's buzzing like a bee. The polka dots are in bloom again. What a pretty pattern.

WAITRESS *(White-trash urban accent):* We got a burger travelin' and a Mr. Potato on a sidecar. Hi, hon, coffee? How ya doin' today? What's it gonna be? Whole wheat, white or rye? Cole slaw or french fried? Anything to drink? Coke. Here you go, Chan, couple of orders at a time. I run this counter like clockwork. By the time they have their cigarettes out of their pocket I get a cup of java in front of their face. *(Ding)* When I hear that bell I run. I don't care what anyone says anything made with cheese gets soggy under these lights. O.K. we got a tuna melt, cheeseburger, tuna on rye, cheeseburger. And to drink? Coffee, coffee, sanka. I have a lot of miles on these feet. I got everything. Corns, callouses, bunions. Real pretty let me tell you. But when my customers come in they know they're goinna get quick courteous service. Not many people give you that at all.

OPERA LADY *(Pretentious actress accent):* Excuse me, miss. Miss. Miss, may I please have a toasted bagel, a fruit cup, and a tea with lemon. No butter on the bagel, please. You see, I'm an opera singer and it creates too much mucous. You see I'm with the 78th Street Upper West Side Opera Folly. It's a very reputable Opera Folly and I'm a founding member. I'm their only female tenor. We're in rehearsal right now for "Carmen" and guess who I'm going to be. Guess. Guess. Guess. Guess. Guess. Carmen! It has my favorite aria. *(Sings)* But I also like pop songs. *(Sings)* My love's in jeopardy, baby, ooh, ooh, tom tom toma tom tom tom. Excuse me miss, but could you turn down the air conditioning, I think it's blowing on the back of my neck. Miss, I told you no butter on the bagel. *(Starting to get mad)*   You don't have any fruit cup! Why didn't you tell me sooner? You've just wasted my time. I'm busy in rehearsal.

*(Medley and frenzy of characters—this blends into a cacophony of all characters until final frenzy—woman switches accents and characters.)*

*(Medley)*

GAME SHOW LADY: Uh, uh. *(Buzz)* Kentucky. Tennessee? I always get that one right.

SPANISH CHA-CHA GIRL: What do you mean you're dancing with someone else Julio? You motherfucker I'm gonna kill you.

VIDEO GIRL: Hey, what's the matter with this machine? I never lose my quarter. Where's the guy?

MISS AMERICA: Let me keep the crown just one more year. I promise I'll give it back. Just one more year.

HOUSEWIFE: I only have paper napkins. I only have paper napkins.

WAITRESS: What do you mean my coffee is bitter? This is a fresh pot. Why don't you go somewhere else buddy?

OPERA LADY: I told you no butter on my bagel. The mucous is already forming. Just get me the check. *(Cough, choke)*

*(Fade lights—frenzy)*

GAME SHOW LADY: *(Buzz)* Don't I get the . . .

SPANISH CHA-CHA GIRL: *(Buzz)* Julio you son of a bit . . .

VIDEO GIRL: *(Buzz)* Hey Rusty, hey watch me now . . .

MISS AMERICA: *(Buzz)* Don't take my crown, don't take my . . .

HOUSEWIFE: *(Buzz)* Napkins, napkins . . . I uh . . .

WAITRESS: *(Buzz)* Coffee bitter, my coffee . . . why I'll . . .

OPERA LADY: *(Sing, sing)* SING

*(Frenzy flip out-shaking-etc. Pause, breathe. After flip-out, woman sits serenely in chair, wash out. Lights up where ELLEN sits.*

*Switch to ELLEN)*

In America, you look around and you see all these images of people who you should be. People with long hair down to their waist, people with eyes that sparkle, people with clever accents, people who tell witty stories, people that have courage, people that make shyness an art form. There are so many images of people to choose from. Sure, I always wanted to be famous. Who doesn't? It's not just from you Ma. It's from the children on their swings, from the old people shrinking in Miami Beach, it's from the magazines, from the posters, from the airwaves. It's everywhere ... everywhere, telling me to have friends I haven't deserved, find lovers to be slaves, keep my phones ringing forever. Isn't that right? Huh, Ma? Don't we all? FAME AND HEAT AT THE TOP. Just like you said. They'll watch you, they'll imitate you, they'll like you, for your hair, for your smile, for your figure. I don't want to be a spider anymore, some slimy thing crawling around people's teeth. I don't want to become saliva that gets spit out. Saliva that lands in the gutter under the feet of witty people. I want to take the magazine images out of my head the way some people take out the garbage. Don't you see Ma? I want the little things, things I can understand. I don't know what to do with the big things anymore, the things I keep tripping over, the couches, the big couches sitting in the middle of my living room that I can't move, that I can't budge until I start crying and screaming for the little things. A piece of corn I can understand, but what is a personality? Huh Ma? What is a personality? So, I said to the Frenchmen in the cafes, the Italians in the gondolas, to the Indians on the reservations, so I said to her, I'm lazy, I'm sloppy, and I have flat feet. Take me or leave me. Hopefully she'll take me.

*(Phone rings. She looks at it. She doesn't answer. Black out.)*

THE END

*Jessica Litwak*

# EMMA GOLDMAN: LOVE, ANARCHY AND OTHER AFFAIRS

Directed by Anne Bogart

Performed by JESSICA LITWAK

Original Music by Person-to-Person
Slides by Barry Schoenfeld
Production Supervisor: Terry Knickerbocker

*Scene:*

*CHICAGO. September 9, 1901. Evening. "DEFINITION OF
ANARCHY" slide is on the wall as the audience enters.*

*(A knock on the door is heard. Knock again.)*
EMMA: Max! MAX?
*(She enters, moves towards the chair. As she puts her suitcase
down, the following tape begins. Throughout the tape she is
taking off her coat and hat, getting out her book, her letters, etc.)*
MAN'S VOICE: SEPTEMBER 9, 1901. Three days ago President William McKinley was shot. The assassin was quickly apprehended. His name is Leon Czolgosz. He has confessed to being an anarchist. He stated that he became an anarchist through the influence of EMMA GOLDMAN, whose writings and lectures incited him to commit this act of violence against the President of the United States. Vice President Roosevelt has stated that the nation will take action to stamp out anarchy all together. A nationwide search for Emma Goldman commenced. In Chicago, homes of several anarchists were raided and six men known to be friendly with Emma Goldman were arrested and charged with conspiracy, but the woman anarchist could not be found. However, this evening the authorities have traced Emma Goldman to Chicago—to an apartment building at 308 Sheffield Avenue. Thirteen officers have surrounded the premises. Fully armed, the officers watch the windows of the third floor apartment and wait . . .

EMMA *(Wiping her glasses)* : The strangest thing just happened to me. I was walking through the crowds with my bag held up to my face, to protect it. So if I got hit, my face would remain unharmed. No scars. I can't believe it, I was protecting my face. Such feminine vanity. What would Sasha say? Hello. I am . . . Smith. E. G. Smith. At least that's the name I've been using recently. This is not my room. This is my friend Max's room. Max has agreed to let me stay here tonight. At the train station there were a lot of men in grey suits. Dectectives. They think you can't tell them apart from the rest. They think they're invisible, the authorities. But I know a police officer when I see one . . .

But tonight I intend to relax. Relax! My lover is in prison and I have been recently accused of conspiring to assassinate the President of the United States. All over the streets they are saying, "Anarchists should be exterminated. Their tongues cut out, their carcasses soaked in oil and burnt alive." Just this afternoon I was riding the streetcar with this charming young lady. She was wearing one of those new hats; it was beige with pears and flowers bouncing about to one side. She turned to me and said, "Have you read the morning papers? This Emma Goldman is a beast. A blood thirsty monster—she should have been locked up long ago." "Locked up nothing," said the gentleman standing behind us, "She should have her heart cut out and fed to my dog." I nodded politely . . . After all, what do I know of Emma Goldman. I'm Smith. Just plain old E. G.

*(Wagner on)*

ASSASSIN OF PRESIDENT MCKINLEY. AN ANARCHIST. SAID TO HAVE BEEN INCITED BY EMMA GOLDMAN. WOMAN ANARCHIST WANTED.

Did I incite him? I don't remember. I only met with him twice. We spoke for half an hour. This poor boy . . . I wonder what drove him to do this thing? He is reported to have said, "I did it for the working people." Sasha also did something once for the working people . . . but the people are asleep. They are indifferent and afraid . . . I promised Max I would escape to Canada in the morning . . . Max says I have no business being in Chicago . . . he says the police are thirsty for my blood . . . Well, things have been worse. After all, Sasha—that is, Alexander Berkman—is in prison—he's been in prison now for ten years. I don't like to think about it. Perhaps I should have a bath, now . . . you know what Max said? Max said if anyone was to come here tonight, I am to say, "I am the maid." The maid . . . Isn't that what they called Joan of Arc?

*(Wagner off)*

Shall I tell you a story? To pass the time till Max comes. Yes. Let's see tonight is September 9th, 1901 in Chicago, America, I am hiding, NO . . . waiting, NO . . . relaxing at Max's house, and I will tell you a little story . . . My story . . . A love story.

EMMA: I was born in Kovno, Lithuania on June 27, 1869. I came to America—to Rochester, New York at the age of 16. I worked in a factory making two dollars and fifty cents a week. I married Jacob Kirshner, an immigrant, who worked at the machine next to mine at Garson's Clothing Works. At this time, all over the country labor strikes were breaking out—the people were demanding an 8 hour day—on May 4, 1887 a mass meeting of workers was called in Chicago's Haymarket Square. It was addressed by several leading anarchist speakers. It was a quiet and orderly meeting until police burst in and began beating people with clubs. A bomb sailed through the air killing several policemen. All of the anarchists were arrested and on November 11, Friday, Black Friday . . . the day I became an anarchist . . . I was walking home from a meeting with my sister Helena . . .

I was walking home from a meeting with my sister Helena . . . We have just heard the news. The brave anarchists have been hanged. One of them has committed suicide in his cell. Helena is crying, and I am in shock. We go to my father's house. I am in the kitchen staring at the tea kettle. Everyone is talking about the news from Chicago. I know they were innocent—five of them dead, arrested and hung . . . I hear a woman's shrill voice from across the room: "Those anarchists were murderers—they deserve to be hung!" One leap and I'm at her throat. They pull me back. "The child's gone crazy." I pick up a pitcher of water and I throw it in her face. "Get out. Get out or I will kill you!" My father slaps me. Helena is crying. My husband walks out of the room. "I know they were innocent! Five of them dead!" I fall on the floor in a dead faint. They put me to bed . . .

I woke up early. My head was clear for the first time. I had the distinct sensation that something new and wonderful had happened to me.

I woke up early. My head was clear for the first time. I had an ideal, a reason for living.

I woke up early. My head was clear for the first time. I had the distinct sensation that something new and wonderful had happened to me. I had an ideal, a reason for living. I decided to leave my husband, and devote my life to anarchism.

*(Blackout. Lights up in prison cell area)*

August 15th, 1889. The day I met Alexander Berkman. I arrive in New York City. It is a Sunday. Very hot. I have the address of an aunt, five dollars, and one small handbag. I am asking directions. I walk all the way from Forty-second Street to the Bowery . . . a tenement on the fifth floor. My aunt and her family crowded into two small rooms. They seem surprised to see me . . .

EMMA:

"Emma, why have you come to New York?"

"Emma, did you really leave your husband?"

"Emma, how do you intend to make a living?"

"Emma, do you realize how hard it is for a woman alone?"

Their voices make me . . . sleepy. They sound like flies buzzing. I have left everything behind me to start a new life. This interrogation is very upsetting. I'm going out for a little walk, I tell them. A walk? It's 95 degrees out there . . . I wander around New York City . . . On Third Street I meet a man I have seen in Rochester. He takes me to Sach's Cafe—a gathering place for artists, and revolutionists and workers . . . we sit down at a table . . . I hear a loud voice: "Bring me an extra large steak. An extra large cup of coffee!" "Who is that glutton?" I ask. "That is Alexander Berkman. He never has much money, but when he does he eats Sach's right out of food. He's a very serious young anarchist. One of those obsessive types. The cause above all else— you know the kind . . . shall I introduce him to you?" We approach the table. He stands up to shake my hand. "Alexander Berkman, Emma Goldman." He is a boy of eighteen but with the neck and chest of a giant. Big shoulders. Brown eyes. Very severe forehead. Somehow a little frightening. We look at each other. "Hello." Very nervous. "Pleased to meet you." I am smiling, I don't know why. I stumble over the leg of the table. He catches me up in his arms. "I saved your life," he says. "Well I certainly hope someday I will have the opportunity of saving yours."

It was two weeks after that, when he was taking me to Brooklyn to meet Johann Most . . . that is the day I began to tell Alexander Berkman all about myself. He interrupted me. "Call me Sasha," he said.

*(Blackout. Lights up on apartment. Tape. EMMA's voice)*

"Men and women, do you not realize that the State is the worst enemy you have? It is a machine that crushes you in order to sustain the ruling class, your masters. Like naive children you put your trust in your political leaders. You make it possible for them to creep into your confidence, only to have . . . "

EMMA: September, 1889. How I discovered public speaking.

Johann Most was a prominent anarchist. He published an anarchist newspaper called *The Freiheit*. It was Johann Most who first recognized my talent. He was the one who convinced me to begin public speaking. I was never so terrified of anything in my life. To this day, I cannot face the stand without a stiff shot of whiskey ... back then, of course, I was new at it—I'd get up to speak at a meeting and when I'd open my mouth, no words would come out ... just a kind of gasping for air—like a fish. This was very embarrassing—but Most believed in my passion. I don't think he had much regard for the revolutionary zeal of most women—he referred to them as "emotional stupids"—but I guess he thought I might be different ... He said he wanted to make me a great speaker to take his place after he was gone ... at first I thought he was making fun of me ... he'd take me out to dinner and we'd drink alot of wine and he'd laugh and toast: "To your first speech, little Emma." He loved to spend money ... we'd go to expensive places and he'd order wonderful things and buy me flowers afterwards ... this made Sasha very mad ... Sasha said Most had no right to spend money on me when the movement was so much in need of it ... Sasha said that it was inconsistent for an anarchist to enjoy luxuries when the people live in poverty. But I had a hard time criticizing Johann Most for anything he did. He was my idol. He was the best public speaker I ever saw ... he could turn a room to flame with the furious clarity of his voice ... I worshipped him, and he loved me. Once he grabbed me in a taxi and kissed me all over my face and arms. He was incredibly ugly, but I let him do it because he was such a great man. I wanted to make him happy. It is amazing to me that just a few years after he got me started on my way, he turned against us . . .

*(Blackout. Lights dim on. Prison cell. Soft music)*

EMMA: 1890. Sasha.

The meeting was over. Sasha and I filed out with the others. We walked home in silence. When we got to the house where I lived ... my whole body began to shake. Like a fever. I looked at Sasha. He came upstairs. I had a very narrow bed. We were squished together in the darkness. He whispered soft Russian words into my ear ... that made me drowsy ... I began to drift into a dreamy sleep ... then suddenly I was roused by an electric current rushing through me ... a soft, shy hand ... trembling ... touching me tenderly ... I reached out for the hand . . . we were in a wild embrace. A terrific pain—like a sharp knife . . . breaking through everything that had been dormant, unconscious and suppressed . . . in the morning I was still reaching out—eagerly, hungrily . . . seeking . . . he was sleeping now . . . and I raised myself up on one elbow and watched him . . . the face of this boy that attracted me and repelled me at the same time . . . he was so hard and yet so tender. I kissed his thick black hair and then I fell asleep beside him . . . That was the first time.

*(Blackout. Apartment: Bright disco lighting. Loud music)*

We are at a dance. I love dancing . . . I'm the wildest dancer in the room—I won't come off the floor. I see Sasha's cousin coming towards me . . . I grab his arms and give him a spin . . . he pulls away from me . . . his face is very serious, as if he's about to announce the death of a beloved comrade or something. "Emma, an anarchist should not be dancing so recklessly—with such abandon. You are on your way to becoming a force in the movement. It is undignified . . . " "Undignified? Who the hell are you to throw the cause up in my face when I'm having such a wonderful time? How can a cause which stands for such a beautiful ideal . . . for freedom from convention and prejudice . . . demand the denial of joy? What, do you want me to become a nun with the cause as my cloister? No, I want to dance . . . and if I can't dance, I don't want to be a part of your revolution." . . . People are staring at me. My voice is too loud. Some people are clapping, but others are shouting . . . I find Sasha's face in the crowd. He is furious with me . . . I know what he is thinking . . . one must love the cause above all else. He is thinking I am selfish and silly and immature . . . but I know what I feel, Sasha . . . I know what I believe. He turns and walks out of the hall. I am alone.

*(Lights dim.)*

EMMA *(Rolling cigarette)*: I had other lovers. One of them was Fedya—Sasha's best friend. Fedya was a painter. One day he asked me to pose naked for him. So I did. In the middle of the painting he had to stop. He said he was too nervous. We became lovers. When Sasha came home, I told him and the two men embraced . . . that night the three of us stayed up talking all night—we made a pact: to dedicate ourselves to the cause—to live and work for ideals and to die together if necessary . . .

*(Blackout. Apartment: Light on EMMA in chair)*

Sasha is upstairs building a bomb.

He's never done it before, but we have a copy of *The Science of Revolutionary Warfare* . . . and it gives a pretty good description.

EMMA: May 1892.

Henry Clay Frick. Big Boss. Carnegie Steel Mills. Wages are cut. Workers strike. Mills close. Workers attacked. Beaten and killed.

Henry Clay Frick. An infamous piece of scum.

Sasha has decided to kill him. Sasha knows where he can get dynamite—from a man on Staten Island.

Sasha says . . . "I have waited all my life for the sublime moment to serve the cause. To give my life for the people." Sasha says although he will live long enough to justify his act in court, he knows he will be condemned to death.

"I have waited all my life for the sublime moment to serve the cause. To give my life . . . "

Oh Sasha. The more you talk, the sicker I feel. I am oblivious of everything else—Cause, Duty, Message . . . what do these things mean compared with the force of our love?—Does our three years together mean so little to you that you can sit there calmly expecting me to go on living after you've been blown to bits or strangled to death? I will go with you, Sasha . . . I can help. Besides, I simply must go with you . . . do you understand, Sasha? An argument ensues. Finally he agrees to let me go with him—at least as far as Pittsburgh . . . on the train.

*(Blackout. Lights up on EMMA in chair. She is sleeping. As the light brightens she awakes.)*

The bomb didn't go off . . . and if the test bomb doesn't go off, that means the second bomb made out of the same materials won't go off either. We have lost forty dollars and a week of our time. Now I'll never be able to go with Sasha—we don't have enough money for train fare . . . we have to raise the money to buy a gun. So how does one go about raising quick cash? How does a woman, alone in New York City, go about raising a large amount of cash quickly? How far does one go for the man one loves? For the cause? Well, I got the idea from Dostoyevsky. In *Crime and Punishment,* Sonia became a prostitute to support her little brothers and sisters . . . and when the men came, she lay on her cot with her shoulders twitching and her face to the wall. If sensitive Sonia could sell her body, if Sasha can give his life to the cause, then certainly I can . . .

EMMA: The question is, am I attractive enough for the men on the street? I look tired. But my complexion is good. I have nice hair. I'm too large in the hips for my age, but I'm a Jew, I look like my grandmother—it's something to be proud of! . . . Anyway, I could always wear a corset and high heels. Oy.

*(Blackout. Lights up on EMMA in chair)*

July 16th, 1892. I am walking up and down Fourteenth Street. I join the long procession of girls I have seen so often. I try to mimic their calm. The weather doesn't seem to affect them. They disappear into doorways with men and then reappear again . . . each time a man comes by me, I get nauseous . . . and then I panic as he passes me by . . . I have to raise the money to buy a gun! It's 11:00 and still I've had no luck. Finally an elderly man in a pinstripe suit approaches me . . . he beckons me to follow him into a cafe. He orders two glasses of wine.

"I don't know what drove you to the streets, but I'm sure it wasn't looseness, or lack of excitement in your personal life."

"Many girls are driven to it by economic necessity!" I told him.

"I'm not interested in economic necessity, or in the reason you were out there, I'll just tell you one thing: There's nothing in prostitution unless you have the knack for it . . . and you most certainly do not." He put a ten dollar bill down on the table. "Now go home," he said. "Don't you want me to do something? Take off my clothes or something?" He smiled. "You are a sweet kid, but you are silly and stupid, and immature." "I was twenty-three last month!" He laughed at me. I ran all the way home. With ten dollars for the gun.

*(Blackout. Lights up on EMMA. Train station at night)*

I cling to Sasha. He is already on the train. I am on the lower step . . . his face is bent low to mine . . . he is holding me: "My sailor girl." . . . the train moves . . . "Comrade, you will be with me to the very last.

Steam. Wheels turning. He loosens his hold and gently helps me down . . . I have to jump a little off the step . . . I'm running, waving and crying after the departing train . . . Sasha, Sashenka!

Arms outstretched. A life is being snatched away . . .

*(Lights up)*

July 23rd. Saturday.

YOUNG MAN BY THE NAME OF ALEXANDER BERK-MAN SHOOTS FRICK—ASSASSIN OVERPOWERED BY WORKINGMEN AFTER DESPERATE STRUGGLE.

I ran after the departing train. We only had money for one ticket. He said only one person was needed for the job. He barged into Frick's office and shot the bastard three times. In the neck, in the shoulder. There was blood. Men ran in. They took the gun. He had a knife. Poison dagger. He stabbed Frick in the leg. They took the knife. He put something in his mouth. They pinned him to the ground. They pried open his jaws. Candy, he said. There was a capsule of fulminate of mercury. All he had to do was chew on the capsule and the whole room would have blown up and everyone in it. They held his head back. They removed the capsule. They beat him unconscious.

Sasha has been in prison now for ten years, many of them in solitary confinement—in a dungeon. And Frick survived and became a hero in the press and the public turned against the workers and the strike was broken. It was said we set back the American labor movement forty years.

*(Apartment)*

I am in the visitor's room in the Western Pennsylvania Penitentiary. I am frightened. I haven't seen Sasha in months. I am waiting and then all of a sudden he's there. In a grey outfit. Looking thin. He has lost some hair. The guard is watching us. I am shaking in the knees. But I keep my hands steady so Sasha can't see . . . ah Sasha. Hello, my love . . . He won't look at me . . . He seems weak. The guard thinks I'm his sister. We sit together on the wooden bench. He has changed. The shoulders hunched, the spirit broken. The brown eyes full of despair. The guard is pacing. Door slams somewhere in the hallway. Sasha jerks his head up. Our eyes meet. I am smiling at him. I don't know why. The guard comes to stand over us. "Your time's up." Sasha jumps to his feet. I feel so helpless. He kisses me, and I feel something pass from his mouth into mine . . . Then he is gone as quickly as he came.

In my mouth was a message from Sasha. It said that I should go to Inspector Reed and try to get a second visitor's pass for the next day. But by the next day my identity had been discovered and no one was in the mood for doing Emma Goldman any favors . . . No, after that day I didn't see Sasha again for nine years.

I went back to live at my aunt's house. No one would rent me an apartment—my name seemed to frighten the landlords. My friends suggested that I give an assumed name, but I would not deny my identity. I was very desolate during those days when Sasha was first in prison . . . I would sit in a cafe on Second Avenue until three in the morning—or ride back and forth to the Bronx on a streetcar . . .

EMMA: Johann Most was a jealous man. He fell in love with me . . . and hated Sasha. When Sasha tried to kill Frick, Most turned against us. He publicly denounced Sasha—saying that Sasha's "dramatic heroics with a toy pistol" were ridiculous and Sasha was doing the movement more good by being locked up on Murderer's row, than he could on the outside . . . Most was denying the very ideas he himself had put forth, in order to make Sasha look like a villainous fool . . . I decided to challenge Most—and to compel him to explain his lies in public. I bought a horsewhip.

I am sitting in the front row of Most's lecture. My whip is under my coat. He gets up to speak. I get up too . . . "I came to demand proof of your insinuations against Alexander Berkman." There is instant silence . . . I hear him mumbling something about "hysterical woman" . . . I pull out my whip and leap at him . . . I get him across the face and then on the neck and shoulders . . . then I break the whip and throw the pieces at him . . . The crowd is outraged . . . "Throw her out! Beat her up!" I ran out of the hall.

*(Wagner on. Apartment. Lights dim. During this monologue, Emma tears up the letters that are in the book and scatters them on the floor.)*

I wonder where Max is? He should be home by now. I only came to Chicago because so many of my friends were being arrested—just for having their names linked with mine. I thought perhaps I would turn myself in but then Max said . . . I don't like to think about it. Sometimes I wonder if my life has been worth living up to this point. Has anything been heard? Has the world shifted even a little? Here I am pretending to be a maid in someone's apartment, getting ready to run off to Canada like a horse thief. I don't know . . .

If you're buried under a ton of dirt, isn't it better to hack away at it with the heel of your shoe rather than turn away from the task for lack of a shovel? . . . Isn't it better to fight for breath than to resign oneself to suffocation? Anarchism is a process, not a finality.

Oh Sasha. I am trying to be brave.

*(Music off. Apartment light fades out as she steps on to platform.)*

Union Square 1893. I was scheduled as the last speaker. I could hardly wait for my turn to come. When it finally did, I got up to speak and my knees were shaking . . .

I step forward. I hear my name echoed from a thousand throats. "Emma! Emma! Emma!" I begin:

"Men and women . . . " Uproarious applause. The clapping seems to me to be like the wings of white birds fluttering. Men and women, we respect your patriotism. But may there not be different kinds of patriotism as there are different kinds of liberty? I know many people, I am one of them, who were not born in this country—nor have they ever applied for citizenship, and yet who love America with deeper passion and greater intensity than many natives, whose patriotism is manifested by pulling, kicking and insulting those who do not stand up when the National anthem is played. Our patriotism is that of a man who loves a woman with open eyes. He is enchanted by her beauty but he sees her faults. So we too, who know America, love her beauty and her richness, but with the same passionate emotion, we hate her superficiality, her cant, her corruption, her mad unscrupulous worship at the altar of the golden calf.

Remember that those who fought and bled for your liberties were in their time considered as being against the law, as being dangerous disturbers and troublemakers. They not only preached violence but they carried out their ideas by throwing tea into the Boston harbor. They said, "Resistance to Tyranny is obedience to God." They wrote a dangerous document, perhaps you've heard of it, called "The Declaration of Independence." A document which remains dangerous to this day.

I may remind you of two great Americans, undoubtedly not unknown to you: Ralph Waldo Emerson and Henry David Thoreau. When Thoreau was placed in prison for refusing to pay his taxes, he was visited by Emerson, and Emerson said to him, "David, what are you doing in jail?" And Thoreau replied, "Ralph, what are you doing outside, when honest people are in jail for their ideals?"

*(Platform. Lights dim)*

I paid the first due for my opinions in 1893 . . . with a year's free residence at Blackwell's Island Penitentiary. I was arrested after a speech I gave at Union Square. They grabbed me as I left the meeting. There were three of them. They held my hands behind my back and pushed me against a wall. "Why am I being arrested?" I asked them. No response. "What am I being arrested for?!" "For being Emma Goldman," one of them replied . . . after that I got so used to being hauled away at a moment's notice by the authorities, that now I always carry a book with me when I go to a meeting . . . that was the worst thing about that first time; I was locked away without anything to read.

*(Prison cell: Lights dim.)*

There are two kinds of cells in most penitentiaries. One is called a light hole, and the other a blind cell, or dark hole. This is often referred to as the dungeon where a prisoner is kept in solitary confinement. It is a damp dark room, 52" by 107", with a small opening 7" long and 1 1/2" wide to let in some air. There is no bench, no window and no source of light. The prisoner receives two pieces of bread and two cups of water per day. I have been sent to the dungeon on several occasions for short periods, but Sasha has been kept in solitary confinement for months at a time.

Anarchism brings man to the consciousness of himself. Will it lead to revolution? Indeed it will! No real social change has ever come about without revolution. People are either not familiar with their own history, or they have not yet learned that revolution is but thought carried into action. Anarchism is the theory of social harmony. It is the great, surging, living truth that is reconstructing the world, and that will usher in the dawn.

*(Apartment: Lights dim)*

I am an anarchist and I do not believe in force—moral or otherwise, to induce you to do anything against your own conscience. Your conscience is the best guide in all the world. If that is a crime, if that is treason, then I am willing to be shot.

*(Apartment: Lights bright)*

I believe in anarchy
freedom
free love
speech
I believe in America
Courage. People. Pride.
I believe

there is great work to do.
Now. How-
ever we can. I believe
that governments abuse their power.
Now and always. I believe
the future is in our hands.
I believe in dreamers.
Children. Streamers.
Confetti. That
dancing is important.
I believe
that if America has entered the war to make the world safe for
democracy, she must first make democracy safe in America.
I believe in peace.
Beauty.
Duty. I believe
people must be free to express themselves
differently
in liberty.
I believe in passion. In art.
In anarchy.
That women must make choices about their lives as wives
mothers
lovers.
That America should not stick her nose into other people's
business.
I believe
in revolution coming next, in
sex
Tolstoy
a brand new age.
Duse on stage.
I believe in Russia's cries,
in open eyes,
the President lies.
I believe in anarchy. In
Freud's interpretations.
Humanity. Salvation.
I believe in action. Strikes.
The likes
of which we've still not seen.

I believe in honesty.
Good food. Wine. Hard work. Happiness. Radiance.
The free child. Oscar Wilde.
Sasha's smile.
Defiance. Pride. I believe
anarchism is a process—not a finality.
I believe in the spark—
a light in the dark.
History is eternal recurrence—and people are still tearing
each other apart
after all these years.
We fools go on . . .
believing
in life. Equality. Freedom.
The American people.
Awakening.
Liberation. Emancipation.
Dreams.
Ideals.
Anarchy
I believe in standing alone, grown
woman. Making her own choices. Her
face held high, not afraid to die.
I am proud of my beliefs and
I believe . . .
no matter what anyone says about me
I believe in the masses
in destroying the classes.
I believe in tenderness in
common sense—the declaration of
independence.
I believe in Max, Johann,
Fedya. Alexander Berkman . . . Ah, Sasha . . .
I believe in anarchy . . . and
Nietzche says:
"That which is born out of love
always takes place beyond good and evil."
Upheaval. Starting fresh.
Making a mess.
I believe in moving.
Not losing.

Hope.
In coping with these hard but wonderful
times.
Lines of people all over the world
Holding each other, helping each other.
Protesting war. Shouting for . . .
freedom, free love, speech . . .
I believe in anarchy . . .
"The philosophy of a new social order based on liberty
unrestricted by man-made law."
I believe in fun.
Running, screaming, dancing, leaping, laughing, kissing,
wishing.
Making it real.
I believe in love.
Again and again.
Women and men. Women
and all the men in my life . . .
I believe in living for today.
Strong. Resilient. Gay.
Paving the road.
I believe our enemy is the dying past . . . and we are the
glowing future . . .
I believe in we.
I believe in me.
You, her, him, them (as long as they're us) not to mention
everybody who
doesn't know
yet . . . I believe in charm.
Strong arms.
The great alarm . . . Sasha still in prison, and
here's to social harmony.
And all the men in my life. I believe in going ahead. I believe
in America.
I disbelieve in authority. Invasion. Coercion and force.
Oppression, violence, marriage, divorce.
I believe in the absence of government . . .
in people running their own lives.
Children. Not deprived
Of love.
Free love. And the freedom

of dreaming . . . and making dreams live.
The pleasure to give
a warm hand
to the next man. Fortified
with courage and will.
Pulling each other up the hill.
I believe in anarchism.
The new world.
Women and men
beginning again. I believe
in patriotism of the soul.
Our role
in the liberation of mankind.
I believe in the spiritual
political
economic
revolution of life. Strife.
I believe in doing whatever it takes
to make
it happen.
*(Apartment. Lights dim)*
It's getting late.
You're probably wondering why I've never had children.
I have an inverted womb.
The doctors say I should have an operation.
But I never have the time.
I love children.
But there's the movement to think of . . .
*(Prison cell: lights dim)*
September 6, 1901. Three days ago.
I am in the visiting room of the Western Pennsylvania Penitentiary. The guard calls in Prisoner A7. A skinny man comes towards me. He has lost all of his hair. The same grey suit. I look into his eyes. He looks away. We sit down on the bench. The guard stands beside us. We try to speak to each other. In Russian. The guard says, "Speak in English!" We try. It has been nine years. He won't look at me. The guard leans over us. "Your time's up."
*(Lights up: Apartment)*
EMMA: Well, if Max doesn't show up soon, I'll go to bed . . . I have a big trip ahead of me in the morning; I don't

particularly want to go to Canada, but I guess it's the best thing. I can't hide here forever using a fake name—especially Smith. I suppose I'll have that bath now . . . there's nothing like warm water to calm the nerves . . . Oh, I'm not frightened. I've had a lovely evening . . . I've torn up all the letters that were likely to involve my friends . . . I've thought of Sasha . . . and I've enjoyed all of this, the stories . . . it's so good to be able to look back, to forgive oneself . . . and to feel proud of the things one has accomplished. But even more, to feel proud of the pain, and the silliness . . . and the lovemaking. These are trying but wonderful times. There is great work to do. Be brave beloved comrades. Our enemy is fighting a losing battle. They are of the dying past . . . We, are of the glowing future.

*(Apartment: Slow fade. During the next taped speech the lights dim as EMMA undresses and gathers the torn letters on the floor, puts them in the bowl on the table and lights them on fire. The play ends in firelight.)*

MAN'S VOICE: At 10:00 on the night of September 9th, 1901, Emma Goldman was arrested for her alleged complicity in the plot to assassinate President McKinley. She was captured at the home of an anarchist friend, Mr. Max Baginski. At the time of the discovery of her whereabouts, Emma Goldman was taking a bath. There was a scratching at the window and then a crash of glass. She emerged from the bath in a house robe, to find an officer clutching the window ledge with one h and, and holding a gun in the other. The apartment, on the third floor of the building, had no fire escape. She reached towards the officer at the window, "Look out, you'll break your neck!" she recalled. He entered the room through the broken window and ran to the locked front door. He opened the door. Twelve officers crowded into the apartment. The chief officer, Captain Schueffler, grabbed Emma Goldman's arm. "Who are you?" he asked. "I am the maid," she replied. "Who lives here?" inquired the captain. There was no response. When further questioned as to the whereabouts of Emma Goldman, the alleged maid claimed to be a Swedish servant girl who did not speak English. The officers completed a thorough search of the apartment, finding no evidence, until one detective discovered a fountain pen on the floor . . . the pen was engraved with the name "Emma Goldman." The captain ordered three of his men to remain on the premises to await the return of the woman anarchist. Goldman realized the game was up. There was no way out. No sign of her friend returning home, no use keeping up her false identity. "Excuse me, officer," she said. All the policemen turned to look at her . . .

EMMA: I am Emma Goldman.

*(EMMA pours water over the flames. Blackout)*

The End

*Denise Hamilton*

# PARALLAX
# (In Honor of Daisy Bates)

Directed by Denise Hamilton

Daisy Bates.............................................MICHELE SHAY

"To give your child for a cause is even harder than to give yourself."
　　　—Eleanor Roosevelt, 1962, in her preface to Daisy Bates'
memoir, *Long Shadows of Little Rock*.

/par–e–laks/n:　the difference in apparent direction of an object as
　　　　　　　seen from two different points.

*Scene:*

*On the darkened stage 2 TV monitors brighten as a news pro-
gram-type music theme is heard. On both TV screens is a program title, NEWS AMERICA, and an unseen announcer speaks.*

ANNOUNCER: News America—brought to you by Tabco,
America's leading pharmaceutical company. And by Computex,
number one maker of computers.

*(On the TV screens appears a man, the TV news program nar-
rator, who speaks.)*

NARRATOR: Good day. News highlights for Monday, May
8th: Fighting broke out again in the Middle East along the border of
Pakistan. Famine continues to affect thousands in Central America's worst drought in history. Yesterday's typhoon in South Central Asia has left its devastating mark in a 1200-mile radius. On the
brighter side, stock prices closed very high yesterday, and Wall
Street had one of its busiest sessions ever.

Now to our feature story. Today on News America we'll
spotlight a person known around the world as one of our country's
most incredible women. A woman whose life has been marred
repeatedly with tragedy, and in the face of personal loss, has remained a monument of strength and courage. She is the matriarch
of America's greatest political family. Today we pay tribute to Rose
Fitzgerald Kennedy.

*(Shattering of glass is heard from stage right as lights rise in that
area; the woman who was sitting in a chair screams and drops to
the floor as a rock is thrown towards her.)*

DAISY *(calling her husband):* L.C.!! Honey?!! *(Slowly she sits
up, and seeing the rock, moves to get it.)* No, L.C., I'm alright.
This was thrown through the window. *(She stands while unwrap-
ping some paper wrapped around the rock, then reads.)* 'Watch out,
Daisy Bates: rock this time—next time, dynamite.'

*(She looks at her husband, then the window, then begins to
sweep up the window glass fragments as the TV monitor
brightens. The TV narrator is seen on both monitors; simultaneously, on a large screen upstage are shown photos corres-*

*ponding to his commentary: pictures of young Rose Kennedy, etc.)*

TV MONITORS

NARRATOR: Thrust into the public eye at an early age as the daughter of one of Boston's most flamboyant mayors, Rose Fitzgerald was destined for the political spotlight. She began as a wealthy socialite; a gifted public speaker who campaigned on behalf of her father. Courted by many, she finally took the hand of Joseph P. Kennedy—who, at age 25, was the youngest bank president in the United States. Joseph Kennedy later became Chairman of the Securities and Exchange Commission, then Ambassador to England, and parlayed his business ventures to amass a personal fortune worth approximately 400 million dollars. A fortune that was to ensure Rose and Joseph Kennety, and their nine children, financial independence for perpetuity.

DAISY *(as if talking to children surrounding her):* You are all very brave young men and women to volunteer yourselves like this. How can I give you any guarantees? Except to say that one day you'll look back on this and know that it was worth it. That you have the right to go to that high school because only then will the state provide you with the proper public education.

That mob that attacked Elizabeth is just a sample of what's to come. Now I'm trying to get some ministers to escort you to school tomorrow. But the crowd will still shout curses at you. They may spit on you, probably try to kick and beat up on you. They see you as a threat. My conscience can't tell you to turn the other cheek. But ... if you can just ... manage somehow to keep to the business of learning, the only thing you'll threaten is their security in being right. People will do a whole lot of ugly because of discrimination. A long time ago my father taught me not to blame the people, but the discrimination that made them do it. I had started hating some girls that I once called my close friends—all because of ... an incident that had nothing to do with them. My father said, "Daisy, you're putting your energy in the wrong place." It took me a while to get that through my head. I hope it won't take you as long as it took me to realize that. So don't waste time hating those people; it won't change them, and there are too many other things to work on that you *can* change ... I'm sure the last thing on a teenager's mind is to be standing up for some cause. I know when I was your age I was busy fussin' over my hair all the time. Trying to make it look like bobbed hair without really cutting it, you know,

'cause the flapper look was in. And I was such a tomboy, too . . .
Thinking about back then, I can remember times when I felt no one
could really understand what I wanted. But it wouldn't have mattered so much if I could have just done whatever I wanted to without
thinking twice about it. Without having to worry about being re-
sponsible . . . Maybe some of you feel that way now . . . If there
was any way that I could do this for you, I would. Tomorrow, my
spirit will be going out with all of you—all nine of you.

*(As before, and from now on whenever the TV monitors come*
*on, the narrator is seen on both TV screens, while pictures*
*corresponding to his commentary are seen simultaneously on the*
*large screen upstage.)*

TV MONITORS

NARRATOR: She is the first mother in history to see 3 of her
sons elected to the Senate and one become President of the United
States. Many wonder how she managed to raise such a remarkable
family of achievers.

*(An elderly woman is shown on TV being interviewed, while*
*Kennedy family photos are on the upstage screen.)*

WOMAN: I was a frequent summer guest at their Hyannis Port
home back in the early years, and it was always very pleasurable.
But the Kennedys didn't flaunt their wealth, nor did they cater to
their kids. The children were given average allowances, much like
your average family. Even though there were 9 kids, Rose tried to
make it as normal a household as possible. I don't think the kids
really knew, while growing up, quite how wealthy the family was,
'cause their parents kept it from them, you see. Rose never liked to
use the word 'wealthy'; she preferred to say they had advantages.
And she taught them that advantages imposed responsibilities.

DAISY *(to the parents group):* Yes, I'm hearing you all; Mr.
Ray, I understand your point. I know you don't want Gloria to do,
but we have got to send all nine of those kids back to that school
again tomorrow. All you parents realize the importance of integration; now we've got to decide if it's going to be this generation or
never. A lot of us are waiting for things to get right, but they won't
get right until *we* fix 'em. The world is looking at us and we have
got to take advantage of this situation, no matter what they try to
stop us with. Yes, Governor Faubus has politicized this thing and
surrounded that high school with state troops, but we can't be in-
timidated. If we don't challenge him, then our lawyers can't appeal
for an injunction against court order interference. It's been three

years since the feds outlawed segregated schools, yet Arkansas has been dragging its feet and no one has challenged it . . . Your children know the risks they're taking; they're all so wonderful. Mr. and Mrs. Eckford, I didn't tell you that those nights Elizabeth slept over she had nightmares about that first day.  But you've talked to her since, and you can see that she refuses to give up. *Just like we must.*

The School Superintendent has strongly suggested that we not accompany the kids, 'cause if violence does break out, it will be easier to protect them. *(pause)* We are all worried about the mob, Mrs. Thomas. Hate groups from all over have landed in this town. They'll be out there tomorrow in full force.  And to be honest, I don't know how the Superintendent plans to protect them. As long as those state troops surround that high school it's off limits to the local police and they can't escort them either. *(pause)* No, Mrs. Eckford, I don't think lynching will happen.  I know its only been two years since that 14-year-old Till boy was lynched, but I think this country is moving away from that. They don't need that tactic anymore.  I don't know all the answers.  I do know that turning back now isn't one of them. *(pause)* Yes, they've made our house a target, that's for sure. Without installing flood lights outside, or Dr. Freeman next door keeping watch with his rifle, I'm sure my home would have been blown up by now.  Make no mistake about it, Mr. Ray, I'm not interested in becoming a martyr. Being president of Arkansas' NAACP, I just want to see this state get up off its ugly behind and comply with the law.

*(Upstage is projected a written statement. We hear a woman's voice reading the statement.)*

SLIDE STATEMENT:  The Arkansas State Press, co-owned by L. C. and Daisy Bates, had Southwestern Bell Telephone, the Arkansas Gas Co., and the State Power & Light Co. as major advertisers.

TV MONITORS

NARRATOR:  That indomitable spirit has seen Rose Kennedy at age 75-plus travel thousands of miles at different stages of her life on behalf of her sons' political careers.  She continually maintained her high energy and drive with social activities, and an avid interest in glamorous fashions, frequently cited for being one of the world's best-dressed women.

DAISY *(putting on her hat):*  And L. C. . . . it was so awful. They were so angry the kids got in safely, they beat up the entire Life Magazine staff on the scene.  Then their photographers were arrested for inciting a riot. Like one of them said, he was arrested for taking his head and hitting someone's fist with it. I've got to head out now; don't let all those reporters eat up everything in my kitchen. I should be back by eight. *(She walks toward the door and is stopped by her husband's words.)* What? Oh, yes. *(She walks with hesitation toward a desk, and opening the drawer slowly removes a gun)* Yes, I guess I should. *(She puts the gun in her purse and exits slowly.)*

*(Upstage is projected a written statement, and the woman's voice is heard reading it.)*

SLIDE STATEMENT: An extremely devout Catholic, Rose Kennedy attended convents in America and Europe.

*(Another statement appears, then the voice reads.)*

SLIDE STATEMENT: In 1951 Rose was conferred the rare title of Papal Countess by the Vatican, in honor of her exemplary motherhood.

ANNOUNCER: This portion of our program is brought to you by TABCO, maker of products for the home. With TABCO, 'your family's needs are our concern.' Back to our program.

TV MONITORS

*(An elderly, professional-looking man with a pipe is being interviewed, with Kennedy family photos on the upstage screen.)*

MAN: To put it simply, she created a very stimulating environment that made her children highly competitive, both physically and mentally. They were always playing competitive sports like football on the lawn, the girls included. They were all expected to excell in everything and to come in first place. It was almost like they were driven to win. Plus the kids were expected to keep up with current events. They practically breathed politics, day and night. The *New York Times* Week in Review section was mandatory reading, and was often discussed at dinner.

DAISY *(coming on stage, she pulls up the chair to sit and talk with the kids)*: Terrence, bring that tray of doughnuts over here. Carlotta, I've got more juice in the icebox if you want. Thelma, because of your cardiac condition we're trying to get all of your classes on the first 2 floors so you won't have to climb those stairs. *(pause)* No, Melba, I'll have them for all of you by next week . . . So, come on, tell me, how was it today? *(She surveys them as no one ventures to speak.)* Well, don't all speak at once. *(more silence, then she breaks into a smile)* They did? That's a very positive sign, Minnijean. I'm glad they invited you to join the Glee

Club; just don't let it interfere with your schoolwork, dear. *(pause)* I know know much of a track star you were before, Jeff, and it's a shame you can't join this school's team—or be President of the Student Council, like before. Knowing that when you decided to transfer says a lot about you, young man ... You've all given up so much, so much. You all have had to learn very quickly how to dodge the punches, too. Nothing could really prepare you for something like this. But you just gotta stick. ... My real mother was murdered when I was very young. They never found out who did it. But years later, one day while I was in town I saw a stranger staring at me. At first I couldn't figure out why he was staring so hard. I knew he didn't know me. Then it dawned on me that he was staring becaue I looked so much like my mother. And that he was probably the man rumored to have killed her. So I walked up to him and stared him in the face. And I could tell that it really bothered him. Really bothered him. From then on I made a point whenever I went into town to walk past the saloon corner he hung out on. To just go stand in front of him—and stare him in the face. And I did that—over and over—for months. Until he finally drank himself to death. ... I don't mean to suggest that guilt plays a part in changing people's attitudes; in fact, it may have very little to do with the matter. It's just that, well, sometimes just *being* there—and refusing to go away—can be awfully effective. So you just gotta—you gotta stick to it.

TV MONITORS
NARRATOR: She is a woman who has given her children up to history. In light of the tragedies she has had to bear, Rose Kennedy in recent years has, understandably, remained private and secluded from publicity. 'It is wrong,' she has said, 'for parents to have to bury their children.'

DAISY *(to her husband):* Well, L. Christopher Bates, long time no see! You actually left the office to come home and eat dinner for a change. *(She smiles, kicking off her shoes.)* It's been so crazy, both of us so busy, not having any time to rest. *(She is massaging her temples.)* Yes, my head hurts a little, not so badly, though. What possessed us to start a newspaper the year we got married? Using all of our savings; were we naive or crazy? *(pause)* A little of both, huh? ... Honey, sit down for a moment ... L. C. ... a woman came by the Press office today while you were out. A white woman; didn't give her name, just said she was representing a Southern Christian women's group. She said that her organization was interested in helping desegregation, but that they needed time. They needed time, she said, so what they want me to do is call a press conference. *(pause)* Yes, a press conference to announce that for the good of the community I will withdraw my support of the school integration plan. If I do that, she said, her women's group would work towards integration—in their own time, and in their own way. I asked her what would happen if I didn't withdraw my support. She glanced around the offices . . . and told me that they'd make sure we'd lose everything. She gave me her phone number to call. *(She pulls out a small piece of paper form her pocket.)* I have until 9 a.m. tomorrow to give my anwwer. *(pause)* No, she didn't seem like any of those crackpots that send us hate mail . . . Maybe she's bluffing, L. C., you know they'll try anything . . . but I'm thinking . . . I keep thinking, too, about that night Elizabeth slept over, her waking up and screaming from a nightmare about the mob attack . . . and still she and those other kids refuse to give up . . . I plan to call this woman at nine tomorrow morning—and tell her that she can just forget about me and any press conference. . . . Tell me I'm doing the right thing, L. C. In risking so much. *(pause, as she looks at him, then replaces the paper in her pocket)* I keep reminding those parents that what we're doing is not just for their children but for all children. Honey, do they realize that I'm just as concerned about their kids as if they were . . . Could we have done more now had we our own children? . . . I guess the State Press has been our baby, huh, L. C.? A 16-year-old child we're devoted to. I remember the birth pains, alright. Let's hope we can both get through this adolescence. *(She shakes her head in wonder.)* Serves us right, running our own business. You told me, "Daisy, if I own the paper I can't lose my job cause no one can fire me!" *(She chuckles as her light dims.)*

*(Upstage a statement is projected, and the woman's voice reads.)*

SLIDE STATEMENT: Four of the parents lost their jobs once it was discovered who their children were.

*(Another statement appears, then the voice reads.)*

SLIDE STATEMENT: Terrence Roberts' family moved to California due to pressure.

DAISY *(to her father):* Here, Daddy, let me fix that cover for you. *(She mimes adjusting a bed cover.)* Why do you say that, Daddy? *(pause, then she nods)* L. C. *is* serious; has he said anything to you? *(pause)* Huh, I don't know about this 'man-to-man' thing; if he's interested in marrying me he ought to speak to me first. *(pause)* Yes, he's a fine young man alright. L. Christopher Bates. You know, he's doing very well in insurance, but he majored in journalism and that's really where his heart is . . . He wants to write for a newspaper someday. *(pause)* Don't try to talk, you'll start coughing again. Ohh, are you alright? Lie back and catch your breath, now . . . With you being so sick you should concentrate on getting stronger, not worrying about me . . . Daddy, listen, please . . . You say you're worried about me, and I'm telling you—don't be. You've tried for so long to protect me in many ways, but that doesn't mean I'm weaker for it. It doesn't mean that at all . . . Remember that time, oh, I guess I was about 8, and it was the first time I got my first smack of 'being colored' by some rude white store owner? I knew when I got home you would fix him. Yes, my daddy would make things right by going to beat up that old nasty white man. When I told you what happened, you told me that there was nothing you could do. That it wasn't that you were afraid of the man, but you had to think of what would happen to me and the family if you did anything. Oh, God, I can't forget that, cause that's when I began to really see you. I've seen all that strength, and all that you couldn't use. Don't think I haven't seen it. Don't be mad at yourself for the times you couldn't stand up and fight, no, no. There are other ways, and other people to fight for you . . . You say you don't have much to leave me? Oh, Daddy, that's not true . . . You once told me I was filled with hatred, and that hatred can destroy a person. Well, I've lost the hatred, Daddy. That hatred about my mama's death is gone, I don't carry it around anymore . . . And don't you worry about me. *(She freezes in place.)*

*(Upstage, a statement is projected, and the woman's voice reads.)*

SLIDE STATEMENT: By the second school semester, the hair of Gloria Ray's 32-year-old mother had turned completely white.

DAISY *(at school board office):* Yes, Superintendent, I'm back again; why was Minnijean Brown expelled? *(pause)* She was retaliating abuses that have been continuously heaped on her by certain classmates!!! Since the paratroopers were removed from inside the school, the state's replacements are turning their heads when our kids are attacked. Naturally she had to strike back, and now she's being expelled for good?! I can't tell you how to run your schools, but it's up to you, not the Army, to maintain discipline inside that building . . . You wrote the first draft for the school plan, you were for it—what happened? I guess they've gotten to you too, huh? Just like they got to the others. Seven ministers said they would support us, only one has come through. So many civic-minded citizens were willing to help; now all of a sudden everyone is either sick or out of town. And I don't hear any more committee talk about "Little Rock welcomes progress." Somehow all those folks in the middle have moved right on over to one side: that easy side where you keep your mouth shut and don't make waves. Look here, Virgil Blossom, you and I both have sat on many a committee. We're both quite familiar with the school board and how it runs. We both know this '3-phase' integration plan is, at best, a disappointment; starting with only 9 children when 350 wanted to enter. You know, politics is a strange thing; in order to accomplish anything you got to do what the power people want you to do, and quite often that means you *can't* accomplish anything. So maybe because you want to be re-elected, you feel you must appease the board. But realize there's a chain reaction taking place, and you're falling right in line instead of taking the risk to speak out. Sometimes it takes just one person in one meeting to get people thinking. Sometimes it's better to accomplish the little you can do now—and risk being fired—instead of being re-elected to do more of nothing. At the very least we expected more assistance from this office; after all, you're the Superintendent of Schools!!! *(pause)* Oh, the teachers have been fine, they try their best to keep things smooth in class. It's what happens in the hallways between classes, and it's that gang of kids being led by that Mother's League. You have the list of abuses. The mental torture of those kids is ongoing. It's a miracle they can concentrate on their studies. Well, I've been to the Pentagon twice. And I'm letting you know that until you decide where you stand, I'll get the Secretary of the Army to provide guardsmen to personally escort each child from class to class—so these attacks will stop. And so *no one else* will be expelled. Do you know there's a group of kids now wearing printed cards that say "One down and eight to go?"

*(On the upstage screen are pictures of the Little Rock school integration incident as the monitor brightens.)*

TV MONITORS

NARRATOR: In this evening's news briefs: twenty years ago today marked the integration of Little Rocks public schools, that historic moment when Arkansas state troops defied federal law and prohibited 9 black children from entering Central High School. In an unprecedented move, President Dwight Eisenhower intervened with 10,000 National Guards and 1,000 paratroopers to escort the children and uphold federal court order.

DAISY *(at a podium):* During my speaking engagements these past few years, I am often asked how I felt that day in 1957 the paratroopers arrived. President Eisenhower had responded to our telegram earlier so I knew what to expect. The kids were all gathered at my house—we had decided they should leave from there. When Minnijean looked out of the window and saw the soldiers coming she said "For the first time I feel like an American. Somebody cares about me." There were 22 soldiers immediately surrounding the kids; 2,300 more with gas masks and bayonets lining the street all up to the school. I was excited the troops were sent, but not happy. Any time it takes 11,000 soldiers to assure nine Negro children their constitutional rights in a democratic society, I can't be happy.

People also expect me to be bitter about . . . my personal life. You see my husband L. C. and I lost our newspaper. The paper's advertisers cancelled their contracts, for no mysterious reason, and with them went sixteen years of our lives. I truly understand the power of advertisers and the control media has in choosing what's presented. Which is why the success of the State Press as an activist paper meant so much to us. We've had all the bad experiences of civil rights workers: being arrested, being threatened, and so forth. However, at some point you pass over the crisis. I don't know why you do. But when you've passed it a lot of things are lost in your new perspective. They're not important anymore. What is important is that through that outrage at Little Rock the world was made to realize the shameful discrimination that has been practiced in this country, even against young children. If they could, most people would just sit back, or be fence sitters. But each and every man and woman can make a difference if he or she believes they can; if they've had someone to help them; one person to tell them they can. We've all got our own resources we can use, to build on, and it doesn't always take money or contacts, but just plain energy that's focused.

Events in history occur when the time has ripened for them—but they need a spark.

TV MONITORS

NARRATOR: And now—back to our special on Rose Kennedy: A Portrait of Strength.

*(The TV monitors fade slowly, as does the portrait of Rose Kennedy on the screen, but the light lingers on Daisy. Finally the stage lights go to black.)*

THE END

*Cynthia L. Cooper*

# HOW SHE PLAYED
# THE GAME

Directed by Bryna Wortman

Eleonora Randolph Sears, Althea Gibson,
Gertrude Ederle, Sonie Hennie,
Gretel Bergmann, Babe Didrickson...............SUSAN STEVENS

Music Consultant: Paul Schubert

*Characters:*

*All of the characters in* How She Played the Game *are real women. As persons from sports history, their very individual stories are dramatized through one actress, who plays all of the roles.*

ELEONORA RANDOLPH SEARS, *one of the century's most versatile sportswomen, ELEO is from Boston, high-spirited and energetic. Born in the late 1800s, she lived through the 1960s, and serves as the play's "moderator."*

ALTHEA GIBSON *became the first Black athlete to break through the barriers of top tennis competition. Although her background as a child of the ghetto made her an unlikely candidate for such a role, her personality did not. We catch up with her on the day she is about to win the Wimbeldon tennis match.*

GERTRUDE EDERLE *was the first woman to swim the English channel, breaking the records of the five men before her. After her highly-publicized channel swim in the early 1920's, Ederle, an unassuming young woman, seemed to disappear from the public spotlight. We see her forty years after the famous swim, when life has evolved in a different direction.*

SONIA HENIE *was the richest athlete in all of history, dying with some forty-two million dollars. Of Norwegian background, she made her fame on ice in the twenties and thirties, and then in movies and her own ice revues. She revolutionized the concept of ice skating by incorporating dance and movement. Hardly an article speaks about her without mentioning her shrewd business skills. We see her on ice as her career winds down and she takes stock of her accomplishments and her future.*

GRETEL BERGMANN *had the misfortune to be Jewish in Germany at a time when Jews were not welcome. A high jumper, Gretel was added to the German Olympic team of 1936, but when the time to compete came around, Gretel was not in the arena. She relates to us the feelings of all those who find their abilities unfulfilled for reasons beyond themselves.*

BABE DIDRIKSON, *became famous mostly for her unbelievable skill at golf, but she had a perhaps more extraordinary career in track and field . . . and tennis . . . and baseball . . . and basketball . . . and . . . It is no exaggeration to say few athletes ever—male or female—possessed the abilities of Babe Didrikson. While naively rushing forward against the societal forces that wanted women to be everything that she was not, Babe exuded a down-home confidence that pushed her to become a star.*

### ELEONORA RANDOLPH SEARS

*(The actress enters, and takes command of center stage. She is in the character of Eleonora Randolph Sears. Eleonora is a Bostonian, well-bred, energetic, and high-spirited, with more than a bit of verve. Her tone is light, and she has a sense of humor and intelligence about her. She whips out a sheet of paper and addresses the audience.)*

ELEONORA: I want you to listen to this resolution they passed about me:

"Whereas it has been brought to the attention of the Burlingame Mothers Club . . . "

They're out here in California where the United States Polo Team is practicing. Frankly, I had every intention of becoming the first woman on the team.

" . . . that Miss Eleonora Randolph Sears . . . "

That's me . . . Eleo Sears, great great granddaughter of Thomas Jefferson—*the* Thomas Jefferson— the Belle of Boston, and voted the Best Dressed Woman of 1910 . . .

" . . . has been parading through our city in the unconventional trousers and clothes of the masculine sex, having bad effects on the sensibilities of our boys and girls; Now be it resolved that we are strongly opposed to this unsightly mannish garb and request that Miss Sears restrict herself to normal feminine attire.

Signed Mrs. D. S. Harns, the year of 1912."

Naturally, I decided to pay a visit to the Mothers' Club. In trousers!

"Dear women. Mothers! Please, sit back down. I have no intention of 'corrupting' you . . . I haven't that much time. This is my unsightly mannish garb. Take a good look, ladies. Because, *this* is the future staring you straight in the corset! Your daughters and their daughters won't stand for being laced up, stowed down, braced against a board! And there's more—women are going to leave these silly parlor meetings and play outdoors! Polo! Tennis! Biking! Hiking! In trousers!"

"Ladies, I will make a stand: Women will excell in ways men have not! Not equal. Excel. And to prove it myself, I offer a bet of $200—yes, $200—that I can walk—without stopping—faster and farther than any man has ever done on record. I will walk—from Burlingame to Del Monte, California! One hundred and nine miles! . . . Anyone willing to take my bet?"

"Well, then, what a pity. . . . Oh . . . Mrs. D. S. Harns, I believe? You accept my bet? Well, what a bully good opportunity. Then arrange for your monitors . . . I will commence at once!"

*(Eleo turns as if exiting, begins to strap on her walking shoes, and addresses the audience.)*

One hundred and nine miles is a very long distance. But, I'm no quitter. I'm off.

Five miles. Ten miles. Twenty-five miles. Around about mile 37.1 I'm feeling a little tuckered out. The future of my career as a champion pedestrian doesn't seem too promising. . . . I promise . . . by George, I promise . . . every time I find out about a woman trying to make a special mark in sports, I will write her a little note. A certain 'hey-ho, bully good' congratulations—good luck from me—Eleonora Randolph Sears. I swear to it on this dusty road at mile 37.2 between the cities of Burlingame and Del Monte in the state of California.

*End of Eleo, seguing into the next character*

ALTHEA GIBSON

*(A musical bridge carries the actress into the character of Althea Gibson. Dressed in tennis whites, hair neatly coifed, she is strong and tough and carries a tennis racquet with a grip that lets everyone know she intends to use it mercilessly. It is July, 1957, and Althea Gibson is about to become the first Black tennis player—male or female—to win the Wimbeldon championship. When she speaks, she talks to an off-stage character,*

*Darlene Hard, another tennis player. Althea opens her locker, finds a letter. It is heard via a sound tape.)*

"Dear Miss Gibson: Old as I am, I can hardly remember a time when I've been as incensed as I am at the way you've been treated at these so-called tennis tournaments. Well, being the first person— male or female—to break the color barrier is a mighty task. I just want you to know you can count on me rooting my heart out for you whenever you play. Sincerely: Eleonora Randolph Sears, July, 1957."

That's nice. That's real nice.

*(Althea puts the note down. She looks up as if someone is signalling her and then calls to Darlene.)*

What?

Darlene, the ballgirl just came by. You hear me? The match begins in fifteen minutes!

*(Althea picks up a tennis racquet, and fiddles with it.)*

It's hot out there, Darlene, honey. Real hot. Nearly a hundred degrees of hot. Folks falling out in the stands. It's so hot they ran out to get blocks of ice to keep the Queen cool. So you take care to splash some cold water on your face before we head out to the court, all right? We got a show to put on for the Queen. Althea Gibson, Darlene Hard . . . two Americans on the grass courts of England.

Me . . . I'm cool like I've never been. This is the kind of hot we had in Harlem. Yay, I'm from Harlem. Harlem, New York City, U.S.A.

Days like today, all of Harlem floats through your memories, pushes out from under your skin like something you can't contain any more. *(Music comes up in background)* If you listen real close, you can hear the music of Buddy Walker's Harlem Society Orchestra drifting by. And there I am on 143rd street, 'cause in 1939 that's the street the Police Athletic League closed off for us kids to play.

*(She acts out the next scene.)*

"We won! We won! The 143rd Street Club won again!"

"Mr. Walker! Mr. Buddy Walker! We took the paddle tennis tournament again!

"Phenomenal? You really thought I played phenomenal? Will you dedicate a song to us tonight?"

"Why do you ask me a question like that? I didn't fight nobody. I didn't have to. I was winning!"

"Shoot, Buddy. I don't 'xactly know *how* I learned to play. I just did. They didn't teach us none at school. That's why I had to quit. And my folks don't care none. That's why I had to run away. Now I just play."

"Would I? Yessir, I would love to play at the Harlem River Tennis Courts club!"

"Yes sir, I surely do promise . . . 'If you take me to play at the Harlem River Tennis Courts club, I . . . promise . . . not to get into any fights.' . . . That aren't absolutely necessary."

I went to the Harlem River Tennis club, where the fancy Negro society played. It *was* different. Everybody was all dressed up in immaculate white and acting so strange, like it was a church meeting or something. I just walked out on the court and played. Pretty soon all the other players stopped their games and were watching me. I felt grand!

"What do you mean 'out'? That ball was right on the line! You tell me to my face that ball was out!"

*(Althea drops her racquet and rushes like she's going to fight.)*

Buddy called me over to the sidelines.

"I can't help it, Buddy! The one thing my daddy taught me was how to box when I need to."

"I understand," he said. "But you don't really know how to fight. Folks have a different way at the club. Everyone acts polite. They shake hands. And then they go out and play like tigers and beat the liver and lights—out of the ball."

*(Repeating that, gently, as if remembering one of the ten commandments.)*

"Shake hands and beat the liver and lights out of the ball."

Not too long after that the two Black doctors saw me play. They thought I was the Black tennis player who could play in the white tournaments and win. So they arranged to take me South, where they were from. I went back to high school. Went on to college. And all the while I worked my tennis game like nobody's business.

*(Looks out as if someone's signalling her)*

What's that? Five more minutes? All right.

Hear that, Darlene? Put a washrag to your head, doll. That'll cool you down.

I want to know if you can hear, Darlene? You see, you're white. Harlem's just a name to you. You're still young. About the age I was when I took up tennis. I'm thirty years old, Darlene. That makes me an old lady for tennis.

*(As if playing the game)*

Last year, the crowd here at Wimbeldon booed me, and it threw my game. This year, I'm going to serve hard, let the ball jump off the grass. I'm going to rush to the net, cut away the volley. And I won't even notice the heat.

Reason I've been telling you all this, sugar, is, you see, the heat makes me feel right at home. I'm going to win. At last. I've got to, hon. See I always wanted to be somebody. So what I'm saying, Darlene, is I'm going out there in front of that Queen today, and I'm going to beat the liver and lights out of you. You can understand that, now, can't you, doll?

*(Calling)*

Yeah. We're ready.

It'll be over soon, hon. Then we'll go back and win the doubles together—you and me. When we go out there, Darlene, I want you to shake my hand. All right, hon?

*(She grabs the note, sticks it in her bag, and turns, with racquet, as if exiting.)*

Yeah. We're ready. We're ready.

*End of Althea Gibson*


GERTRUDE EDERLE

*(Actress takes on the character of Gertrude Ederle, who in 1926 became the first woman to swim the English Channel. Music, once again, serves as a bridge between characters. It is 1969 now, and she is 62. Gertrude Ederle is a matronly woman and hardly seems athletic. She is pleasant, and a bit shy. Everything about her seems straight-forward, reflecting perhaps her parents' New York-German heritage. She is extremely hard of hearing. In an outfit that indicates swimming—goggles, nose-plugs—Ederle carries a scrapbook out of the locker. She looks up as if seeing someone. When she first starts speaking, she shouts.)*

HEY! I REMEMBERED THE SCRAPBOOK FOR THE CHILDREN.

WHAT?

*(As if someone has pointed to her ear. The actress quickly puts in a hearing aid.)*

I don't mean to blast you out. I take off this silly hearing aid before the swimming class with the deaf children.

*(Finishes adjusting hearing aid)*

I'm always afraid of scaring folks off when they find out I'm practically deaf. I told my fiancee back—oh, 40 years ago—back in 1929—I said, "Now that all this channel swimming's made me deaf, sweetheart, I bet you don't want to marry me." 'Course I was just joking. And he looked at me and moved his lips very slowly, so I could read what he was saying. 'I do believe that's the case, Trudy,' he said. And you know, I never saw the man again.

*(She laughs at this.)*

Now, then. Here's the photographs. My Olympic medals. Letters.

*(A letter falls out)*

Oh, yes, I remember this one.

*(She half recites the letter. Sound on tape)*

"What a bully accomplishment to be the first woman to swim the English channel! And to beat the records of the five men before you by over two hours! Gertrude Ederle, believe me, I write with my best wishes for your speedy recovery and hope you will not have any regrets."

Ach! Regrets? Can you imagine? *(She laughs)* Do I have regrets?

*(Trudy pulls off her hearing aid, puts on a red swimming cap. She speaks dreamily, as if stepping into a completely different world.)*

I wore a red bathing cap. And a black swimsuit, with a silk flag of the United States right on it. It was the same suit I wore at the Olympics in 1924.

*(It is the day of the channel swim. Ederle talks to William Burgess, who is her trainer.)*

'Before I start off, I want to thank you for serving as my trainer on the channel swim, Mr. Burgess. Having somebody who's made the swim gives me courage.'

*(She starts rubbing on jellies, as if a routine chant.)*

'Olive oil, first. Lanolin second. Then, the special blend of petrolatum and lard.'

'But I got something to say, Mr. Burgess. You know, I tried last year and the people in the boat pulled me out before I got across.

'Yes, sir, I know twenty-two miles is a long distance in the ocean.'

'Yes, sir, I know it's bad weather conditions and there's powerful currents . . . and jellyfish . . . and that the water temperature is only 57 degrees.'

'I *know* it took you nineteen tries before you made it yourself. But Mr. Burgess . . . my father's a fruit merchant. I couldn't afford coming over on the steamer, or training, or paying for the escort boat. I had to take on a commercial sponsor. You know that means I won't be able to go to the Olympics again. That's a lot to give up, Mr. Burgess. That's how much I want to swim the channel'

'I know the people in the boat think they're looking our for the swimmer. But, Mr. Burgess, you're not a member of the Women's Swimming Association we have in New York City. You saw the Victrola they installed in the boat? With my favorites—*Yes, We Have No Bananas*—and *Let Me Call You Sweetheart?*' They want me to make it!'

'There. I think I'm all greased up.'

*(Starts shaking out limbs, making final adjustments.)*

'The point is, Mr. Burgess, you're going to be in the boat with the reporters and photographers and I want you to know I am not coming out until I walk on the beach in England. Don't try to pull me out. The Women's Swimming Association is counting on me.'

Once you're in the ocean everything else disappears. All of a sudden, there's nothing but what's inside yourself. The water washes over you. The waves crash from the right and the left and from the front and the back. Some of them are eighteen feet high, seems like they're going to swallow you. And all you can hear is the roar of the water, in every direction, until it feels like it's in you and not that you're in it. You know then that you're all alone with the ocean . . . just you and it.

Three miles to go. I hear a call over the rush of the water from the boat. Mr. Burgess.

'You've got to give up.'

I can hardly believe what he is saying. I let his words roll off me like the waves and I threw myself into the water for more of it.

At 9:40 p.m., on August 6, 1926, I walk out of the ocean in Kingsdown, England with the English channel swim record.

*(She laughs)*

They were so sure I wouldn't make it that they had already printed an editorial. "In contests on physical skill, speed, and endurance, women must forever remain the weaker sex." Ach!

*(Ederle laughs, shakes her head, steps back out, puts on her hearing aid. She picks up the scrapbook again.)*

Oh, there were hard times afterwards. The nervous breakdown. The slip . . . my back was in a cast for four and a half years. And I suppose it's true, Gertrude Ederle is not exactly a household name.

*(Looks at letter)*

But do I regret it?

Have you ever heard that song . . . *Let Me Call You Sweetheart?*

*(She hums, sings it a bit.)*

You see, I came back home, and I was the sweetheart of all of New York City. They had the biggest ticker tape parade ever for me . . . Gertrude Ederle, the daughter of a common German immigrant. Two million people filling the streets, flooding it until it looks like the ocean, and cheering for me until it sounds like the roar of the waves. They were throwing confetti from the buildings, and I rode down the street in a brand new car and held my arms out to them. Oh, I suppose it's true they have forgotten me now . . . all those people. But, you see . . . I shall never forget them.

Ach. I have to go and start the lessons. You see, once I teach the deaf children how to swim like champions in the ocean, they shall not forget me.

*(She folds the letter in half, snaps the book shut, takes off her hearing aid, humming and singing slightly.)*

'Let Me Call You Sweetheart . . . '

*End of Gertrude Ederle*

SONIA HENIE

*(Actress takes on the character of Sonia Henie. She speaks softly, with a slight Norwegian accent, almost dreamily. Sonia Henie has an air of confidence, and while somewhat shy, her presence seems to fill the room. It is about 1951. Sonia Henie is 39 years old. With a musical segue, she whirls around as if skating before the audience.)*

My skates shimmer across the ice, turning into the final spin of the Dying Swan routine. As always, I push my weight to the tips of my toes, poise my hands very exactly, and whirl. Eighty times around, they say. But somehow, it is not the same.

It seems as if my whole life has been spinning by. Today: —letters from fans, interviews, a call from Nils, and practice. Always practice.

Since I am six years of age, I have never even been a week off skates. My first Olympics at eight. Now, enough trophies to fill a vault—over 1400. And my ice extravaganzas. And the dozen movies. And the book *Wings On My Feet* that tells the storybook life of Sonia Henie: athlete, champion, star.

Nils' voice on the phone brings back memories from Oslo. He has taken up art collecting; I should join him, he says. I have my own art, I answer. Ice dancing, the way I introduced it to the world 30 years ago . . . that is an art.

I arch my back into the spin. The girls in the crowd are a rainbow of colors. They have collected the Sonia Henie dolls and the Sonia Henie mufflers and mittens and buttons. They have at home the Sonia Henie Pleasure Ice Skates because they want to be like me with a storybook life. They have collected me.

The spin says of its own when it is done. The motion slows, the balance becomes more difficult. I lower my arms and descend into the sit spin.

Then, it is over. The applause begins. I stand, take my bow. But, my smile is from the outside only. Suddenly I understand— patterns carved on the ice are soon gone, the way spring erases winter.

I sweep the ice once more, and make a plan. It is time now for my spring. A picture is forming in my mind: "The Sonia Henie-Oslo Museum of Art." *That* will last.

I have decided. Sonia Henie will spin no more.

*End of Sonia Henie sequence*

MARGARETHE "GRETEL" BERGMANN
*(The actress takes on the character of Margarethe "Gretel" Bergmann. Music serves as a bridge. Gretel is rather ordinary-looking, with dark hair and eyes, strong legs, and a solemn, but not strident, appearance. She speaks with a German accent, and looks up at the audience, as if it were a group of athletes.)*

We do not so much choose to be an athlete. It is just what we are. And the times when we are what we are—an athlete—everything comes together—the body and the soul, the heart and the mind —as we race across the dirt of a track, blood rushing, feet flying.

I was always crazy for sports! I played on the boys' teams. In 1930, I won six track and field ribbons. I was determined to be a World Class Athlete.

So I set my sights on the university in Berlin . . . to become a teacher of physical education.

*(In the next scene, Gretel speaks to an unseen school administrator.)*

"Guten dag. I am Fraulein Gretel Bergmann. I have looked over the list of registrants for the university, but I do not find my name."

"Yah. I have my acceptance letter right here."

"I do not understand when you tell me something has changed. My record is good."

"Chancellor Hitler has said not to admit Jews?"

"How long must I wait for the 'climate' to change? I wish to continue sports. Now. In my best years."

"Yah. Yah. I understand there is nothing you can do."

I would not give up athletics so easily. I went to England. The London Polytechnic! It was a very good thing: I won the blue ribbon in the high jump, 1934! I *was* a World Class Athlete! And my father was there to see it happen.

*(The next sequence is a dialogue between Gretel and her father.)*

"Papa! Hug me! I am the champion in all of Britain!"

"Gretel," he said to me. "I have business to discuss with you."

"What do you mean, Papa?"

"Hitler has made the Olympics of 1936 very important. The Americans are threatening not to come to Germany because of discrimination against the Jews."

"I have heard, Papa."

"Hitler is determined about the Games. He wants all German Jewish athletes to try-out."

"But I have left Germany, Papa."

"You *are* the best Jewish athlete—male or female."

"But, I can't go back now . . . I have a future . . . "

"Gretel. They make threats. Against the Jews. Against the families."

"Yah, Papa. I understand. I understand."

I went back to Germany. Twenty-one Jews were 'invited' to try-out for the Olympics. Of course, we could not train in the same way as the Aryan athletes . . . but we worked hard all the same. In 1935, I was the only athlete declaring Jewish heritage left on the team.

Soon the newspaper stories came:

"Miss Bergmann, Jewish high jumper on German team . . . Change in Nazi philosophy to admit Jews! American boys will have their 'birthright of competition.'" And so on and so on.

But I was busy . . . working out, running, jumping. In June —only two months before the Olympics—I equalled the high jump records! Five feet—three inches! Everybody on the team buzzed that I would win a silver or a gold.

There was an air of excitement everywhere in Germany about the Olympics that summer. Even the Jewish shopowners were allowed to fly the flag for the Olympics! A big parade was scheduled; the very first Olympic torch was going to be lit. All of Berlin had a spit-polish shine. Soon, the word came: the Americans set sail! The big Games were practically on!

In July—July 16, it was—two weeks before the Olympic Games—I received the letter from the German sports authorities. "Fraulein Bergmann. This letter is to advise you that your achievements have been inadequate, and we have found it necessary to remove you from the German Olympic team. Please depart from Olympic training grounds immediately."

So. I was an athlete with no place to compete . . . no 'birthright of competition.'

But at the medal ceremony in Berlin, all the German athletes were required to wear a swastika and raise their arms in a Nazi salute. They even said the words, 'Heil Hitler.' It bristles against the bones. That I could not do. Sometimes . . . it is easier on the conscience not to be an athlete, after all.

*End of Gretel Bergmann*

BABE DIDRIKSON
*(With a musical bridge, the actress takes on the character of Babe Didrikson* (also known as Babe Didrikson Zaharis) *Babe Didrikson seems tall, although she is only 5'6". She is angular and has a magnificent body. Her Texas roots show in her voice,*

*as does her homegrown education and a certain kind of naivety
mixed with egotism. She picks up a letter, and glances at it.)*

What in the hell is this one? From Boston. To 'Mildred Didrikson.'

*(Tears it in half)*

Don't call me Mildred! It's Babe. Or any of them other names
the reporters dreamed up. Like 'Muscle Moll.' That was one. Or
'Texas Tornado.' 'Terrific Tomboy.' Or 'Whatta Gal.' They got
to liking that one. Far as I'm concerned, it's just Babe. Named me
Babe right in Beaumont, Texas.

See, this one day—in 1920 I reckon when I was about nine—I
walked out to the baseball diamond where the boys was playing.

*(Actress acts out the next scene, as if walking onto a baseball
field, grabbing a bat.)*

I picked up one of them bats and signalled the fella that was
pitching to throw me a few. He didn't really want to and twisted all
around on the mound. Well, I whacked that ball good. He pitched
the next. I whacked that ball even harder. Now he winds up and
throws me the best pitch he's got, and I whacked that ball the
hardest anyone ever had on that field. 'She hits like Babe Ruth,'
one of the boys called.

*(Signals for more pitches)*

'I might hit like Babe Ruth,' I said. 'But, I might hit a whole lot
better, too.'

Gals in Beaumont weren't supposed to be nothing like that. In
high school, the girls were mostly in the Miss Purple Club which
was something organized to 'encourage our boys in athletics to
victory.' Shoot. I wasn't any Miss Purple, and no Miss Purple
was 'encouraging' me when I scored 106 points my very self for the
girls' basketball championship.

It was about then that I knew Beaumont wasn't enough to hold
me. So I went off to Dallas to play basketball for the Golden
Cyclones of the Employers Casualty Company. And that's when I
found out about track and field.

1932 was about the biggest year for track and field because of
the Olympics coming to Los Angeles. The competitors were to be
selected at the AAU meet in Illinois. I couldn't hardly sleep the
night before. Mrs. Hall, the escort, had to call a doctor out because
I had stomach cramps so bad. But in the morning, it was one of
those days in an athlete's life when you feel you could fly, you feel
you're a feather floating in the air.

At the stadium, I went right up to the man in charge.
*(In this sequence, Babe speaks as if she is carrying on a conversation with an invisible person.)*
'I'm here to represent the team from Dallas.'
'No, sir, there's just me to represent the Dallas team.'
'I don't care if there's twenty-two girls on the other team. I can whup them all.'
'What *event* do I want to enter? *All* the events.'
'Well, if the most anyone could possibly do is eight, then that's what I'll do. And the name's Babe, sir. Don't call me Mildred.'
I walked out to the stands and Mrs. Hall was the only one I knew.
'Cheer for me,' I said to her. And while I was warming up, I could hear her:
'Go, team, go.'
*(Actress at this point tries to get the audience to join up in a cheer. The actress does stretches, warm-ups, and then demonstrates each event as she announces the winner.)*
The rest of the day went pretty fast. They announced the results over the loudspeaker after each event.
'The hundred yard dash—all winners from the Illinois team. The discus throw, fourth place goes to the Dallas team.'
And then finally:
*Winner* of the shot put: The Dallas team, that is, Mildred—or Babe—Didrikson.'
Well, pretty soon, that feeling I had in the morning that nothing could go wrong started a-growing. 'Cheer for me Mrs. Hall,' I called.
'The broad jump winner is . . . Babe Didrikson. First place in the baseball throw with a world's record, Babe Didrikson.'
'A new world's record in the javelin with a throw of 139 feet, 3 inches, by Babe Didrikson. Jean Shiley has established a new world's record in the high jump and that's just been matched by *Babe Didrikson!* Winner of the 80 meter hurdles in 11.9 seconds, a new world's record by . . . Babe Didrikson.'
By the end there I didn't need to be asking anybody to cheer for me . . . they just did. 'Go Babe Go.'
*(Actress tries to get audience to cheer.)*
I only had me three hours there at the AAU national meet, but when I left, they gave me six gold medals. I broke four world

records. And I whupped the other team of twenty-two women by thirty points to 16.

After I won me three medals at the Olympics, I went back to Beaumont. They had a big parade there for me. And all of the Miss Purple Club was out there a-cheering for me.

You know, folks say I go about winning these athletic games because I have the cooperation thing that has to do with eye, mind and muscle. That sure is a powerful lot of language to use about a gal from Texas. All I know is that I can run and I can jump and I can toss things and when they fire a gun or tell me to get busy I just say to myself, 'Well, kid, here's where you've got to win another.' And I usually do.

I say that even today. To George, my husband. And to Betty, my good friend. Even to the doctors. You see, I done all kinds of sporting events. I won every golf competition they had for women. I was going to enter the U. S. Open, which no woman had ever done, but soon as the papers printed that, they pretty quick passed a new rule that no woman *could* enter. One time a reporter asked me if there was anything I *didn't* play. "Yeah," I said. "I don't play dolls."

I guess around my forty-second birthday, they come to diagnosing me with cancer or some such thing. But I told those doctors three things. I said, I don't care what it is you call cancer, you just make sure my golf clubs sit over there in the corner of the hospital room as long as I'm here to see them.

And don't be calling me, Mildred. The name's Babe.

And you cheer for me, you hear?

*End of Babe Didrikson*


ELEONORA
*(The actress reverts to the character of Eleonora Randolph Sears. She is walking, as in the beginning.)*
Eighty miles. Only twenty nine more to go. Eighty-five. Ninety. I'm walking. Feeling delirious. And, my God, I'm still making promises. Every mile or two. I can't even remember what half of them are anymore. But I'll promise anything if only I can finish.
*(Aside)*
I'm desperate to win that bet.

Wait! There's something ahead! A dusty old signpost and . . . a horse carriage . . . and a little crowd of people! The hell with promises! I'm in Del Monte! *(Damn!)*

*(She yells.)*

"Ladies of the Mothers Club! One hundred and nine miles! Nineteen hours and fifty minutes! I made the goddamn record! Yes indeed! And you ladies look at me. Because I *promise* you with all the strength of womanhood, one thing: I am the future. We will play the game. And this is how."

*(She points to her trousers, music up, strides off stage)*

THE END

*Susan J. Kander*

# MILLIE

Directed by Carol Tanzman
Millie.............................................................LOUISE STUBBS

*Character:*

MILLIE *is a Black woman of 45, though she might seem younger were it not for her extreme exhaustion. Her hair is styled, not fro'd, and was dyed auburn a little too long ago. During the play, she is getting dressed for a night out, applying make-up and jewelry so that by the end, when she exits, she looks fabulous.*

*Setting:*

*Millie's bedroom, representational, parts of furniture, just enough to suggest a vanity with mirror, the headboard of a single bed, a bedside table. Two chairs, one for the vanity and one beside the bed. There is space beyond or outside the room where Millie can move to, and lighting changes help take us to different places in her mind.*

*Time:*

*Saturday, early evening, early summer.*

*(Lights up on an empty bedroom. Millie enters wearing a bright print sack of a dress and houseshoes, her face the picture of fatigue. She carries a can of Coke and a can of orange soda with a straw in it. She walks around what we understand to be a bed, and puts the orange soda on the bedside table, adjusts the straw, and blows a somewhat perfunctory kiss to the occupant of the bed. As she walks back around the bed to the chair, she snaps open her Coke.)*

You think somebody's trying to tell me something or something? They done smashed up my car now for good and all. Can you believe it? Every car I get, somebody feel they got to smash it up for me. Now I got to find me another one, and I got to ask Mr. Lewis to help me out. God I hate that. But I got to get myself back on rubber again, and soon. You know I was thinking, while I was serving the rolls around the table for the tenth time—now why she got to go and have a sit-down brunch the one Saturday I got big nightime plans? Anyway, I was thinking, you know, about getting me a Mack Truck, so instead of peoples running my car all the time, I can get to tearing up some other peoples' cars! *(laughs)* Oh Honey, I am almost too tired to laugh, and you know that's serious! . . . Shoot, now I got to go out tonight in Sam's old raggedy car. And even worse, I got to let him drive. I never let him drive my car. I got not interest in passing it around for other peoples to smash it up for me, hell no. I just said a sweet word, didn't I, baby? Specially, furthermore, since Sam like his whiskey and I only drink Coca-cola, ain't that right? I have a Coke and I smile. What you bobbing your big head around for, Honey? It's the truth. Pop pop pop? Oh, okay, yeah, you right, I drink Orange Pop. Yeah, so do you, so do you. Shit, you didn't get to be over two hundred pounds sitting up in that bed drinking ice tea! You like it when I say sweet words, don't you? You like this dress? Mrs. Lewis brang it to me from Hawaii.

*(Crossing to vanity)*

She never bring me candy no more, old spoil sport. "It's for your own good, Millie; you know it." No I don't know it. Sam love me, he said, just the way I am. Yeah, and I believed him so much, I started doing his damn laundry for him. Like the last thing I need in the world ain't more folks' dirty clothes.

*(Begins to apply make-up)*

This morning I got to work, Mrs. Lewis look at me and said "Millie, you look like death warmed over. Did Honey keep you up all night again?" Like you had your seizures on purpose or something. "Why don't you go upstairs and take a nap?" Seem like she can tell by my face when you've had a seizure in the night, or messed in your bed. She look in my face, at the ring around my eyes, see I'm so tired I could cry. And *then* she says "You look like death warmed over." Dear God, is that necessary? . . . Boy, Honey, one of these days you're going to have one too many. That's how Dr. Brackett says it works. . . . Oh, she's only trying to be nice, I know. She don't sleep too good neither, sometimes. Yeah, someday I am going to say to her "Hey Mrs. Lewis, didn't you get no sleep last night? Now we both look like a corpse reheated!" *(laughs)* See how she did that for Good Morning. Shoot, I think if I did it once, I'd want to do it every damn day: drive in the damn driveway, walk in the damn door and fall into the damn bed. I just said a bunch of sweet words now, didn't I? I always could make you laugh, couldn't I? Always and always. . . . Yeah, that used to be my only complaint about Sam: he may be a old raggedy man, but he never let me get my rest at night. *(laughs)* Now he's dumb enough to think all he's got to do is take me to see Teddy Pendergrass at the Uptown Theater and I'm going to start doing his laundry again? Shit, what kind of a dumb ass broad does he think I am? Now that was a couple of sweet words there, Mildred. A couple. . . . Sure is nice, though, have a man around, for whatever the need arise. . . . That was a long time ago, that first time: a long time. A lot more done changed in old Teddy's life, God bless his heart, than in mines. His life took a real dive: mines just stayed on the bottom of the ocean where it's been ever since you started growing that thing up in your head. Poor Teddy. I can't picture you in no wheelchair, man, not you with your beautiful voice and that beautiful body and the way you use it ooh boy!

*(Music has slowly come up of Teddy Pendergrass singing, and Millie rises, starts moving to the music. Lights change, we go with her.)*

I can still see him, Honey, moving his meat to the beat ooh yeah. Teddy Teddy Teddy, put your meat on the beat boy and move it over my way. Ooh yeah. That man can do it to me any old time he want—ain't you the most stunning man I ever been in the same room with, never mind—oh never mind there's all the rest of the crowd here cause it's just you and me, Teddy, you and me. Oh yes! Ain't you . . . simply . . . stunning . . .

*(Music out, lights return to before, spell is broken.)*

I should have known Sam was low class right from the beginning when he offered me my choice between last row at Teddy Pendergrass and ring-side seats at All-star Wrestling. I knew he wanted me to choose wrestling, too! Almost did, too, just to make him like me. But I got hold of myself. I said "Mildred, what are you doing? He's giving you a choice: choose right." You would never of pulled that kind of stunt, I know that. You would of said "Kick off your houseshoes, Sugar; we are stepping out." Like you did remember when you took me to the Mark IV and we dined and we danced all night long—. . . . Listen to yourself, Mildred. Eleven years and listen to you. Dear God. Well, nothing stops the sand, Baby. Someday, somehow, it'll be better, ain't that right? . . . That was the first time I ever slipped out on you, long after the first surgery. I don't think it troubled Sam none, in fact I know it didn't. But it troubled me plenty and I wasn't going to do it for no All-star Wrestling! Not even Gorgeous George versus The Stomper! Yes, I said The Stomper, Honey, he's our man, yes I know; Millie know. No, it ain't on now; You already watched it today, come on at noon, remember? You watched it with Charles, when he come by to give you your lunch. It ain't on again 'til Monday.

*(She has returned to vanity, and resumes with make-up and jewelry.)*

Perry'll be by later on after I go. He'll sit with you watch the ball game, okay? Give you your dinner. He called me yesterday, asked could he come by and see his daddy, since he didn't feel like going out on no hot dates. *(laughs)* That old Perry. My baby some smart kid, ain't he? Smart? He's downright crafty. Twenty-three years old, junior college graduate, and ain't got no babies! Ain't even shacking with no one; and furthermore, ain't even looking for it. Now that's a crafty kid. Must of took a good lesson from Charles and Tony and all they babies. But imagine that, Honey: of all my boys, my baby a college graduate, working two jobs, money in his pants and ain't got no one to spend it on but his own self. And his old Mama, of course. He gave me these earrings, remember? And for no good reason, neither. Didn't even want me to feed him dinner or nothing.

*(Fetching shoes out of a closet)*

I can't believe it. I told them all three a million times, and you heard me say it: "You make babies, you keep them at your house. I'll visit, on Sundays, after church. Put your lady on the pill; wear a raincoat; do whatever you got to do cause I ain't bringing up your children. I'm tired." Now what do I get every morning but BANG goes the screen door and "Hey Grammaw, got any chocolate cake today?" (laughs) That baby Tony is so fat already, he's just a little butterball . . . I'll never know what went right with Perry, but he's as free as an eagle that boy. I ain't been that free since I was dragging the chair up to the cupboard and reaching my dirty little hand into Mama's sugarbowl. And even that wasn't free, cause she sent me out to pick my own switch for the whipping every time! *(laughs)* . . . . Your mama ain't sent so much as a pair of pajamas in eleven years. She don't care if I was to put you away in a nursing home. And she sure as hell ain't about to help pay for it.

*(Sitting beside bed, putting on shoes)*

Dr. Brackett started in about a home before you was even out of the hospital the first time, all 67 pounds of you. But he dried up about it when you started gaining weight for me. Then, after the second surgery, and the strokes, couldn't nobody understand you but me, and I said to him "How's anybody going to understand him when he's asking for his orange pop, or for the channel to be switched, or trying to tell somebody he done stooled in his bed again? No thank you, he stays home with me. I got my boys to help me out. They call him Daddy, you know, ever since we got married, me and Honey. So he stays home. . . . Two major surgeries, more strokes than I got fingers, and now all these seizures: Lord, Honey, how much can a person put up with huh? Ain't you tired yet? You got nothing left hardly but a mouth, and not even one good eye. Ain't you plain tired? How many more nights like last night, Honey, huh? I can't afford enough sets of sheets for you, and I get so tired of doing laundry in the middle of the night. Dear god, when are you going to get tired? Just plain wore out? . . . .No, why would you? All you do is sit up in that bed all day, watch TV and eat up my kitchen. You're happy. . . . You know, you don't even look like the Honey I married . . .

*(Rising, going back to vanity)*

I guess I don't look too much like the Sugar you married any more, now, do I? These black bags under my eyes. Hair needs touching up. I don't like my roots showing like that. Honey? What do you really think about this dress? Kind of makes me look like a . . . billboard, don't it? *(laughs)* I want Teddy to think I'm sexy.

*(She puts on a belt that transforms the dress from sack to dynamite.)*

And old Sam can just run it out his ass if he say one damn word that ain't a compliment about this dress. I know I said sweet words, but that's okay, it ain't Sunday yet. No sir, it ain't Sunday yet. I got all of Saturday night just waiting for me and Teddy. And then I'll think about Sam, old two-timing lizard. He just got to stay cool and wait for me, cause I promised myself I'm going to take myself backstage afterward and personally wish Mr. Teddy Pendergrass the best of luck and God bless him for the rest of his life. They better let me in back there, too: anybody get in my way I'll just sit on them—Boom!

*(Lights changing, she is leaving the bedroom and going backstage at the theater.)*

Cause I'm going to see my Teddy, tell him "I'll drive your wheelchair any time you in town. You just keep singing, Mister; you keep on living, cause you can't afford to stop turn around look behind you, see how nice things used to be. You just keep your eyes going forward; look on ahead now. You keep singing your songs cause I want to hear them. I always want to keep hearing them, Teddy, you understand me? Always and always . . ."

*(Lights return to normal, she is back home.)*

Never look behind you. Never ever. That's what I'm going to tell Mr. Teddy Pendergrass when I see him tonight backstage at the Uptown Theater—

*(She hears something, turns abruptly to the bed; Honey is having a seizure.)*

Oh shit! Don't fall out the bed, I can't get you up off the floor! God dammit!

*(Runs to vanity, searches the drawer for a box of individually wrapped tongue depressors. A car horn honks loudly offstage.)*

God dammit! Not now, Sam! Tonight! . . . No more! . . .

*(She finds the box, wrenches it from the drawer and spills it on the floor. Drops to her knees to clean up the mess and find one depressor. She is frenzied.)*

I can't do this no more! Too many! . . . Perry . . . Teddy . . . Teddy in your wheelchair!

*(Doorbell rings. Millie freezes with the stick in her hand, there on her knees. Lights change.)*

*(Almost as if in a dream)*

That's what I had to tell Dr. Brackett the other night at that party I did. "I seen you leave the buffet table, Doctor. You so embarrassed to see me you going to pass up my best rack of lamb with sage dressing rather than let Millie serve you? Well here. I brought you a plate, so I can tell you straight out once and for all: I see your eyes, I know what's in your heart, and you got it all wrong. This is me, Mrs. Clinton Gladies telling you Don't you feel sorry about what you done. Now just don't. I know you said six months, but you gave me eleven years with Honey I wouldn't of had without you, and even though you had to cut out some of the best part of him, what you left was more than I would have had otherwise. So don't you ever regret operating on him. *(laughing)* Besides, how could you know I'd be such a miraculous nurse? And he'd be such a hard-headed man? So you see, I'm not sad; I'm happy. This is a happy face, Doctor: a very happy face."

*(Doorbell rings again. Millie comes back to the present, finds herself on her knees with the unused stick in her hand. She looks at the bed, then hurries to it, trembling.)*

Honey? . . . Oh you made it, baby, you made it through again. . . . That's right, sleep. You sleep.

*(Relieved, she turns, but sees now that he has messed in the bed during the seizure.)*

Oh, dear God!

*(Doorbell rings)*

Sam? Sam!

*(Doorbell rings in response)*

Keep your pants on you old coot!

*(She finds a clean set of sheets in the closet, starts to unfold them to remake the bed. She stops. Long moment, then)*

Mildred, you cannot do this now.

*(She puts sheets down, goes to vanity, gets pencil and paper, writes.)*

"Dear Perry. Sorry, I *had* to go. Leave dirty sheets for me. . . . *(Drawing smile face)* Smile."

*(Walks back to bed with note)*

. . . You know, Honey, even if we'd of never went to see that old judge at all, you know you'd be right here, right now. Right here in this old bed, in this old room, in this old raggedy house; with this woman taking care of you. Cause you're my Honey, and I'm your Sugar. Ain't that right?

*(Doorbell rings long and hard)*

Get off my bell you old moose! I'm coming!

*(Putting note on sheets, she goes to vanity, checks herself again, pulls herself together, takes up pocket book, starts to exit. Stops, blows Honey a kiss, takes a deep breath, looks straight ahead, and exits. Fade to black.)*

*Curtain*

# TOUR DE FARCE
## A New Series of
## Farce Through the Ages

### THE PREGNANT PAUSE or LOVE'S LABOR LOST
by Georges Feydeau
translated by Norman R. Shapiro

Hector Ennepèque, first-time father-to-be, is in extended labor and protracted comic convulsions over his wife Léonie's imminent delivery. Before the baby's arrival, this hilarious farce gives birth to multiple comic harangues all aimed at the helpless henpecked husband. When Hector tries to rebound from the recriminations of his aristocratic in-laws, he is swatted aside by an Amazon midwife who takes charge of everything.

A brilliant tableau of conjugal chaos by the master of the genre.

Cast: two males, four females. One set, interior
$5.95 (paper) 96 pages, 5½ x 8¼
ISBN: 0-936839-58-9

### THE BRAZILIAN
by Henri Meilhac and Ludovic Halévy
translated by Norman R. Shapiro

Two amorous actresses are out to capture the affections of a wealthy Paris producer. The wily Micheline spreads the rumor that Rafaella is being courted by a murderously jealous Brazilian. But her plot backfires when, instead of cooling his passions down, the producer's interest heats up. Micheline is non-plussed when the tempestuous Brazilian suitor actually shows up at Rafaella's house. The mad improvisation which follows is a romp in the best tradition of door-slamming French bedroom farce.

Cast: two males, three females. One set, interior
$5.95 (paper) 96 pages, 5 x 7
ISBN: 0-936839-59-7

# The Brute and Other Farces
# by Anton Chekhov
# Edited by Eric Bentley

## "INDISPENSABLE!"
*—Robert Brustein*
*Director, Loeb Drama*
*Center*
*Harvard University*

The blustering, stuttering eloquence of Chekhov's unlikely heroes has endured to shape the voice of contemporary theatre. This volume presents seven minor masterpieces:

**HARMFULNESS OF TOBACCO**

**SWAN SONG**

**MARRIAGE PROPOSAL**

**THE CELEBRATION**

**A WEDDING**

**SUMMER IN THE COUNTRY**

**THE BRUTE**

*128 pages, 5½ × 8¼*
*(paper) $5.95*
*(cloth) $14.95*

## APPLAUSE
THEATRE BOOK PUBLISHERS

# Nineteenth-Century American Plays
# Edited by Myron Matlaw

**"BRAVO! ESSENTIAL FOR ALL THOSE INTERESTED IN AMERICAN THEATRE."**

—*Brooks McNamara*
*Director*
*The Shubert Archive*

From Broadway to Topeka these four smash hits were the staples of the American dramatic repertoire. Their revival in this landmark collection will once again bring America to its feet!

**MARGARET FLEMING**
James A. Herne

**THE OCTOROON**
Dion Boucicault

**FASHION**
Anna Cora Mowatt

**RIP van WINKLE**
Joseph Jefferson

*272 pages, 5½ × 8¼*
  *(paper) $8.95*
  *(cloth) $18.95*

# ERIC BENTLEY'S

## Once Again The Editor of
## THE MODERN THEATRE Assembles The

---

## THE MISANTHROPE and other French Classics
## Edited by Eric Bentley

THE MISANTHROPE Moliere
English Version by Richard Wilbur

PHAEDRA Racine
English Version by Robert Lowell

THE CID Corneille
English Version by James Schevill

FIGARO'S MARRIAGE Beaumarchais
English Version by Jacques Barzun

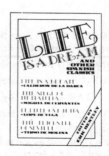

ISBN: 0-936839-19-8
(paper) $7.95
320 pages, 5½ x 8¼, Notes

---

LIFE IS A DREAM and Other Spanish Classics
Edited by Eric Bentley. Translated by Roy
Campbell

LIFE IS A DREAM by Calderon de la Barca

FUENTE OVEJUNA by Lope de Vega

THE TRICKSTER OF SEVILLE by Tirso de
Molina

THE SIEGE OF NUMANTIA by Miguel de
Cervantes

ISBN:0-87910-244-6 (paper) $8.95 (cloth) $18.95
304 pages, 5½ x 8¼, Notes

# DRAMATIC REPERTOIRE

## THE CLASSIC THEATRE And
World's Great Drama For the American Stage.

---

## THE SERVANT OF TWO MASTERS and
## Other Italian Classics
## Edited by Eric Bentley

THE SERVANT OF TWO MASTERS Goldoni
English Version by Edward Dent

THE KING STAG Gozzi
English Version by Carl Wildman

THE MANDRAKE Machiavelli
English Version by Frederick May and
Eric Bentley

RUZZANTE RETURNS FROM THE WARS
Beolco
English Version by Angela Ingold and Theodore
Hoffman

ISBN: 0-936839-20-1
(paper) $7.95
272 pages, 5½ x 8¼, Notes

---

BEFORE BRECHT: Four German Plays
Edited and Translated by Eric Bentley

LEONCE AND LENA by Georg Buchner

LA RONDE by Arthur Schnitzler

SPRING AWAKENING by Frank Wedekind

UNDERPANTS by Carl Sternheim

ISBN: 0-87910-229-2 (paper) $8.95 (cloth) $18.95
272 pages, 5½ x 8¼, Notes